GIFFORDS CIRCUS COOKBOOK

Nell Gifford & Ols Halas

Photography by David Loftus

Hardie Grant

QUADRILLE

In loving memory of Nell Gifford

MENU
the moon hits your eye like a big....
talk to me! (George)
please report to the
CIRCUS SAUCE

CONTENTS

GIFFORDS CIRCUS

FOREWORD

I have tremendous respect for young chefs taking risks to make their dreams a reality. Giffords' Circus Sauce is cooking in the traditional sense. No blobs, no foams – just classic British food served in a unique circus style. Head chef Ols Halas and his team believe in the romance of the dining room and in this case a dining room in a travelling circus tent. This restaurant moves every week or so. The kitchen, tent, tables and chairs all have to be packed and set up again in time for another service in a different field, park or village green. The team scours the new area to create menus chosen according to the produce available from the local businesses, smallholdings and hedgerows. This book, written by Ols and Giffords Circus founder Nell Gifford, is a hymn to this nostalgic adventure through the English countryside.

I was fortunate to stumble upon Giffords many years ago when I happened to be in the same restaurant – Pino's in Marlborough – on the evening of their staff party. After an eventful evening, I was invited to the show and for dinner at Circus Sauce. The show is not just like stepping into another world, but also back into your childhood – the clowns, jugglers and tightrope walkers, and the sweet scent of candyfloss and popcorn. The circus ensemble creates a truly unique charm that only Giffords seems to be able to deliver. During the post-show dinner (a hearty rib of beef with trimmings), I agreed to come back later in the season to cook, out of the kitchen wagons, with Ols, for the entire crew. It was very well received and my love for the circus grew further.

Ols is very rock and roll; he's a chef who takes great pride in the dishes that he produces, presenting his rustic and extravagant feasts just like the performers do in the circus tent – with flamboyance and showmanship. Over the years, I've kept in touch and watched Circus Sauce grow in both achievement and acclaim. It makes me proud to have watched Ols develop into an accomplished traditional chef and to have been there to offer advice and support when he's needed it.

Giffords Circus is the perfect setting for a restaurant, as Nell Gifford's magical circus world has captured the hearts of all who have had the pleasure of seeing it. Nell and Ols have created the most wonderful book by weaving their circus stories together with the recipes that are at the heart of Circus Sauce.

I raise a glass to you both, Ols and Nell, and look forward to this next chapter in your adventure.

MARCO PIERRE WHITE

THE STORY OF A TRAVELLING RESTAURANT:
CIRCUS SAUCE

An army marches on its stomach.

Giffords Circus was started by me and my husband Toti Gifford in 2000. Our costumes are handmade. Our animals are trained by us. Our sets are painted in the barns on our farm. We burn the midnight oil to conjure new visits for the show. It is all we do. Circus is our job, our life, our love. Come to Giffords Circus and be part of the magic.

I remember the moment when we realised that there was scope to open a restaurant alongside the circus. It was in 2000 or perhaps 2001. The circus was standing in Minety, a sleepy village in north Wiltshire. The ground belonged to Toti's aunt and was a farm as well as a proper old-fashioned riding school with hedges, a dusty outdoor school and a stone farmyard full of dozing ponies and happy children.

My brother and his wife had come to stay and I remember cooking asparagus for after the show. I took the roasting asparagus from the little wagon oven and in that moment, I couldn't find anywhere in the crowded wooden wagon to put the hot enamel dish. I ran down the wagon steps onto the field and put the scorching enamel dish on the long grass and thistles. Toti, my brother and his wife were sitting outside. I think I pretty much served the asparagus straight from the dish, sizzling on the grass. The freshly roasted food, the long grass, the sun setting over unruly Minety hedges, the traffic sounds from the busy Malmesbury to Cricklade road, the tent, the anticipation of food, the excitement of the show filling the air – it was a classic after-show circus dinner, and seemed to be something that other people would enjoy.

That little kitchen in mine and Toti's first wagon worked hard. Wagon kitchens are like galley kitchens – you have to be ruthlessly well organised and tidy. Everything has a place and no space can be wasted. It had a four-ring gas cooker and an electric oven, which of course only worked when the wagon was plugged into the generator. It had a little sink and one cold tap so washing up was done by boiling kettles or boiling water in saucepans. The problem with boiling kettles is that the kettle and the oven could overload the generator, causing the whole wagon to trip and lose power, so it became an automatic habit to be continuously boiling water in pans whilst cooking. There were two cupboards for food and two shelves for pans. The kitchen was the first room that you came to at the top of the wagon steps and it measured about eight by five foot – tiny!

On 'build-up' mornings – that is, when the whole company (about 25 people in those days) were putting the tent up on whichever village green or field or pub garden we were playing on – I used to cook eggs and sausages served with tea and buttered bread. Grubby hands and high-vis jackets and bright eyes smudged with last night's make-up and tiredness. In many ways the main fuel of the circus is enthusiasm and a certain determined non-conformism – circus people can be unruly and singular, even stubborn in their self-governance – and a circus company can be hard work to run. We found that hospitality went a long way and I have always tried to have the attitude that everyone on the show is, in a sense, our guest for the season and should therefore be catered for and made welcome. This has been a part of the life of the company, alongside the hours of hard graft – whether that's driving the lorries or putting up the tent, swinging from a trapeze or selling popcorn.

So before the days of Circus Sauce, that tiny first kitchen cooked breakfasts, Bolognese for a ska band visiting from Soho to play on our opening night, dinners for friends and families, raucous cocktails on the last night. In 2008, in Cirencester, the ground was so waterlogged that the hippy French band that season took to paddling from caravan to caravan in a canoe, and the whole ground was covered in roll after roll of straw. Everyone had a cold or a cough; the back tent was flooded. We stayed open even though every outdoor show in the South West had been cancelled and as a result we did a great business. I ran a bar outside our wagon on the last night and it was called 'The Full House Bar' named after the success of the season, and Toti's Shire horse called Full House. That little wagon kitchen was where we cooked for ourselves through the touring summer and also through winter.

Circus Sauce was from the beginning a travelling restaurant. It was perhaps in inception like the cantinas that used to spring up alongside Napoleon's travelling army – a kind of renegade, organic inevitable off-shoot of a group of travelling people.

IN MANY WAYS THE MAIN FUEL OF THE CIRCUS IS ENTHUSIASM AND A CERTAIN DETERMINED NON-CONFORMISM.

Food is sourced locally, but because it is a travelling restaurant, 'local' changes from week to week. One of the first chefs to work at Circus Sauce was a rapscallion chap from Minety called Lance Edwards. Lance used to bomb about in an open-topped MG. He drank copious amounts of Champagne and was always organising outlandish adventures for the circus company. I remember once that he booked us a hot-air balloon flight. The balloon took off from Westonbirt Arboretum. Lance was as enthusiastic as ever, with bottles of blowing bubbles and the odd bottle of Champagne hidden in his bag, bubbles cascading out over the basket of the balloon as we drifted across north Wiltshire. We eventually landed with a thump somewhere around Brinkworth, the basket tipping and spilling out a ragged bunch of circus people. We walked back across the field to the gate and the good-natured farmer was there to greet us, saying "I had heard that you were in Minety next week"; he assumed that the hot-air balloon was our method of travel.

Lance used to make allotment salads – I loved those: big bowls of sharp and hot leaves from local allotments, once memorably dressed with jelly babies. The anarchic tone set by Lance and his front-of-house manager Robbie – who married the girl working in the wardrobe (a sleek New Yorker in the UK at an art school reading fashion) and moved with her to America where they still live with their baby – set the tone for Circus Sauce. It still survives to this day and I love it. Circus Sauce is completely un-precious about its food. It is food to feed an army and served with maximum entertainment. Lance and Robbie used to cross-dress, swap accents (a New York accent came very easily to Robbie) and throw outrageous parties in the restaurant where all the company – Cossacks, New Yorkers, stern Russians and English girls – would end up dancing on the tables under the dripping canvas outside the rickety wagons.

Those early hair-raising days (I remember once, for example, the entire publishing staff of Bloomsbury arriving for dinner in Hay-on-Wye as the chef's assistant set out to forage the hedgerows for that evening's supplies) have slowly changed into a slicker, faster operation led by head chef Ols Halas. He heads up a team of 12 young, hardworking people who, week after week, move the entire restaurant from site to site, establishing a network of suppliers all over the South West. But the vaudevillian nature of the restaurant has not been lost, and between the main course and pudding Ols and his crew stage a puppet show from the restaurant wagon windows. A send-up of the main show, they devise this bawdy production themselves, with the Godfather of Giffords

LANCE USED TO MAKE ALLOTMENT SALADS -- I LOVED THOSE: BIG BOWLS OF SHARP AND HOT LEAVES FROM LOCAL ALLOTMENTS, ONCE MEMORABLY DRESSED WITH JELLY BABIES.

Cal McCrystal in the background offering the odd note but mainly surprised and utterly delighted by their rude, joyful humour.

Foraging is still an element of this summer season. In May at Fennells Farm, the circus HQ, they gather wild garlic for pesto and soup. Strawberries are picked at the PYO farms across the Cotswolds. Elderflowers for juice and nettles for soup are picked from the hedgerows or donated by friendly gardeners along the way, such as Matthew Rice in Bampton; there is even the odd anonymous allotment delivery. The allotment at Chiswick House & Gardens in July provides an array of salads. The butchers across Gloucestershire are now firm friends of the team, including Taylor and Sons in Minchinhampton and Andrews in Marlborough. The restaurant travels on through the summer to Cirencester at the back end of the season, when the mists hang all around the dark tent and at Circus Sauce the public feasts on cottage pie and apple crumble. TE Gifford provides pork for the restaurant and this is served with masses of sage from Nell's herb garden back at HQ.

Alongside this very English seasonal menu, the circus company itself exerts a completely different culinary influence. The circus company is made of troupes and individuals from all over the world, and of course they bring with them their culinary traditions. Barbeques are an absolute mainstay of circus life – random tables and chairs gathered outside caravans, and bags of sodas and vodka, cooked meats and pickles appeared. The Hungarian horseman or Csikós rider cooked goulash in a big cauldron over an open fire for an entire season. There was the unforgettable Ethiopian New Year, when the 14-strong Abyssinian troupe cooked all day in cauldrons outside on open fires, producing a dazzling array of curries, served late at night in the big top, one brother arriving from London with the essential pancake-like bread.

The arrival of the Cubans in 2017 brought with it the mojito, and the Cuban signature stew, the cardeza, a meat stock-based vegetable stew served piping hot with lime juice squeezed into it. Outrageously good! These types of dishes work so well with Ols' intentions – big, hearty communal dishes to feed an army, inventive and joyful, celebrating the global village that springs up wherever there is a circus.

ELDERFLOWERS FOR JUICE AND NETTLES FOR SOUP ARE PICKED FROM THE HEDGEROWS OR DONATED BY FRIENDLY GARDENERS ALONG THE WAY... THERE IS EVEN THE ODD ANONYMOUS ALLOTMENT DELIVERY.

NELL GIFFORD

FROM A FRENCH CHALET TO A KITCHEN WAGON IN THE COTSWOLDS

I first ran away with Giffords in 2013.

I was working in the French Alps when I received a message from an old friend asking: "Do you want to join the circus?" What else could I say but "yes"! At that point I didn't know in what capacity I'd be needed, as I couldn't perform any tricks that I could think of. It turns out it was the very same circus I had seen as a child on Minchinhampton Common where I used to fly kites, back in 2000 when I was 11 years old. They needed a chef to run a travelling restaurant that followed the big top for the summer. The circus toured through the towns and villages I grew up in and around, so I knew all the local smallholdings and vendors to buy produce from. I was sold.

I arrived at Folly Farm shortly after my return from the mountains. The image shall forever stick in my mind: I wandered down the driveway lined with burgundy painted wagons, Ukrainian acrobats practising on the lawn, Ethiopian jugglers throwing several clubs between them in front of an old, quaint farmhouse with a large stone barn attached. I was shown through the hefty oak doors, past a hustle of whirring sewing machines, woodwork tools blasting out sawdust and the muffled sound of musicians rehearsing in the next room. It was exciting, exhilarating and so different from my years of working in the depths of kitchen dungeons. In the corner of the barn next to a large fireplace there was a larger burgundy wagon with a kitchen inside. There was a small oven, a sink and a fridge: this was now my home.

I quickly learned that I would have to adapt if I was to survive the season. I was master of one trade and became jack of all else, knocking stakes into the ground, connecting water and gas bottles, erecting tents, driving vehicles and even performing.

IT WAS EXCITING, EXHILIRATING AND SO DIFFERENT FROM MY YEARS OF WORKING IN THE DEPTHS OF KITCHEN DUNGEONS.

MENU

HAM HOCK "EN CROUTE" WITH
SAUCE GABRICHE & PICKLES...

SMOKED HADDOCK "CULLEN SKINK"
WITH BURNT LEEKS & BROWN SHRIMP...

PEAR & BLACKCURRANT "BIG TOP" WITH CREA

I got to know the performers over the next few weeks: Tweedy the clown, Maxi the Argentinian magician, the Serbian musicians and the French tightrope walker, to name a few. They seemed almost average off-stage – bohemian yes, but you'd never figure what these people could really do! Then I saw the show. The new friends I had just made turned into the most wonderfully talented performers I had ever seen, throwing fire, jumping off horses, flying through the air on a rope or quite simply making me laugh until I felt sick. I was immediately and unequivocally hooked... Hooked on the circus, the lifestyle, the parties, the wagons, the places, and most of all the people.

I used to watch Keith Floyd and Rick Stein on TV when I was younger, obsessively dreaming of eating my way around the world in weird and wonderful places. The Circus Sauce restaurant gave me a chance to do this in the local area. Then, once the season is over, I and the team travel around a different part of the world. We've been all over on our winter breaks and we return ready for the season with just our backpacks, a couple of quid and a host of new ideas to throw at the circus diners.

Touring has since become my life. It's a unique lifestyle you couldn't experience anywhere else and one that's very difficult to give up. We now have a fleet of kitchen vehicles and move from ground to ground, pitching up with chefs who wield sledge hammers, erecting the restaurant canvas, the tapestries, oak tables and candelabras before setting off to find the best produce in the area to serve for our feast at the circus. The communal and hedonistic style of cooking has led us here. Don't just cook – have fun and put on a show!

I WAS IMMEDIATELY AND UNEQUIVOCALLY HOOKED... ON THE CIRCUS, THE LIFESTYLE, THE PARTIES, THE WAGONS, THE PLACES, AND MOST OF ALL THE PEOPLE.

OLS HALAS

CHAPTER ONE

ART IS LOVE

The Giffords Circus headquarters is on the top of a hill on the outskirts of Stroud, called Fennells Farm. This is *Cider with Rosie* country: deep valleys and huge woods. Art and design are embedded in the DNA of this region. There are farmers' markets, radical print houses, live music venues, embroidery studios and, in the ancient farmlands beyond Stroud, there are artists' houses, resettled Londoners and farming families. The area has a strong spirit and a cheerful acceptance of the off-beat, the esoteric and the experimental. We could not have found a better home for Giffords Circus.

Fennells farm consists of a series of steel-framed farm buildings that have been converted into offices, meeting rooms, a library, a woodwork room, a paint studio, a huge costume-making room with storage for 2,000 costumes, some steel-working studios, a vast vehicle workshop and a farmhouse. This last has a central room with a long oak table down the middle and an open fire at one end.

All winter, from October to March, a small team of people work for Giffords Circus on site: two mechanics, a head of transport, a designer, a social media manager and two producers. There are acts to be booked, visas to be applied for, a new show to be planned, wagons to restore, costumes to design, horses to look after, lorries to be serviced, chickens to train. People often ask me if I am taking a rest "now the tour is over", but the winter never feels like a rest. In fact, if anything, we all look forward to the long, warm days of summer – and, although life on the road brings with it a multitude of responsibilities, it at least has a certain restful quality, given that everything is essentially up and running. The winter months are a time of budgeting and searching, a constant drive to improve on the previous year's work. Once on the road, a circus has a life of its own; winter is for the critical planning work.

In January, February and early March, the paperwork, planning and discussions seem endless. Then suddenly our year seems to tilt: the pace changes, the days lengthen, the ground dries and circus people start to arrive. Horse trainers, acrobats, jugglers and gymnasts arrive from Ethiopia, Cuba, Portugal, Sicily. They bring with them their props: swings and crashmats, or gymnasts' bars and cables to be rigged, elastic aerial straps and swinging trapeze bars. There is a cacophony of languages. The artists bring their families and their homes – huge caravans and lorries full of washing machines, bicycles, paddling pools and barbeques. These are people who travel the world working in various shows, and their caravans and vans

ONCE ON THE ROAD, A CIRCUS HAS A LIFE OF ITS OWN; WINTER IS FOR THE CRITICAL PLANNING WORK.

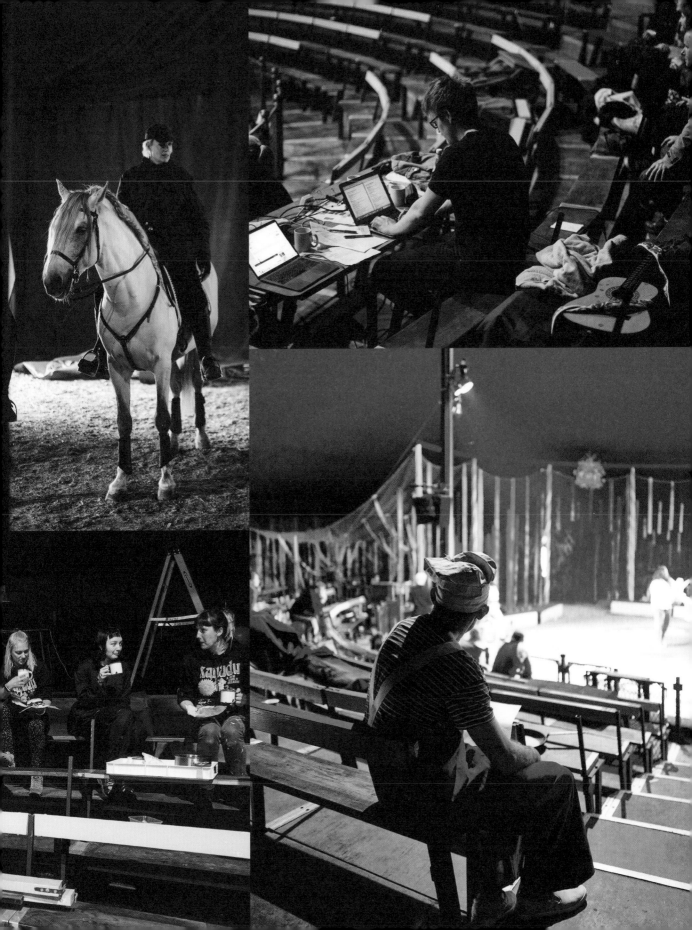

are not temporary arrangements but much-loved, fully equipped family homes. The Giffords Circus company is not only made up of circus artists, though. There are musicians – session players who bring their instruments and a suitcase of clothes. There is a team of technicians who lay endless cables, rig lights, frown into laptops and switchboards, and who stand around the generator having inscrutable conversations about power supply.

We rehearse for three full weeks at the farm, and the countdown to the start of this time is as tense as the lead-up to any opening night. A full company on full pay for three weeks is a sizeable cost, and we can't lose a moment. We have to be focused, ready for opening night, and yet we have to stay open and playful, able to move with diversions and the problems and rethinking that inevitably happen in rehearsals. It is a terrifying but compulsively absorbing activity – one where, quite literally, the world outside and all concerns other than the show become irrelevant, for a few weeks at least.

Our director, the much-loved Cal McCrystal, bombs down from London in his shiny black Mini, swiftly followed by his assistants. They will have their work cut out keeping up with Cal's free flow of ideas and a technique that consists of getting people to derive the most pleasure from the show. Inevitably, the running order will be upended several times over the weeks, and your worst work will become your best and vice versa.

The English musical director James Keay might be seen walking up the hill from Stroud train station in his long wool overcoat, white vest and gum boots, reading a book of poetry as he walks. Choreographer Kate Smythe, trim and glamorous, flies in from the south of France, and our Greek designer, Takis, arrives with cutters and sewing-machine operators. There are magazine stylists, make-up artists and hairdressers. There are carpenters and painters, graphic designers, printers, sign writers, sculptors, plumbers, electricians, circus agents and a couple from America to advise on the operation of the human cannonball. There are photographers and a small team from the BBC World Service recording an arts documentary about circus, plus four teachers and a group of local school children doing a project. There are four yurt builders putting up yurts for 20 or so art interns. In the stables, equine dentists and vets work their way through the circus horses. Within a few days, there are a hundred or more people living and working on the farm. And there is one absolutely vital question: what on earth are all these people going to eat?

THE FIRST MORNING OF REHEARSALS STARTS WITH PORK BELLY BUNS AND A SCOTCH-BONNET-LACED MUG OF HOT CHOCOLATE FOR ALL, BEFORE OLS AND THE TEAM HEAD OFF INTO THE WOODS IN SEARCH OF WILD GARLIC TO FLAVOUR THE KILOS OF CASH-AND-CARRY PASTA THAT WILL BECOME THE MAINSTAY.

Head chef, Ols, sets up Circus Sauce in one of the barns: it consists of two lorries with a seating area under a canvas awning. Behind them is another tented area for gas bottles, crates and bins. Inside the kitchen there are ovens, gas rings, fridges, sinks and stainless-steel work benches, as well as a walk-in fridge and freezer. The whole thing is powered by a generator and fed water through plastic piping. It is from this kitchen that the assembled circus production crew are fed, and it is an exceptionally busy time for Ols as he has to train his new team, plan menus and build and mend the kitchens, as well as feed the cold and hungry circus army on a bootstrap. (Giffords Circus is financed by ticket sales and receives no outside sponsorship or funding, so the operation is run very tightly during rehearsals when ticket sales have yet to really take off.)

The first morning of rehearsals starts with pork belly buns and a Scotch-bonnet-laced mug of hot chocolate for all, before Ols and the team head off into the woods in search of wild garlic to flavour the kilos of cash-and-carry pasta that will become a mainstay. In spring, the farm is cold, the days are long and the work is demanding – it is a time of frugal, resourceful catering. Ols makes pease pudding for the band, down in Stroud rehearsal rooms, and a spread of cakes for Cal's tea party – strongman cake, lemon and lavender cake, toasted seed and treacle flapjack, cookies and pies. Hearty suppers of toad in the hole and, if the weather is nice, an evening barbeque where friendships are formed and plans are made for the summer ahead. In their spare time, the chefs lift weights and prepare jars of homemade pickles and preserves, ready for the coming tour.

SCOTCH BONNET HOT CHOCOLATE

> Hair on the chest without the booze! Keep the bonnet in the saucepan for longer if you like a bit more heat, but forewarn your unsuspecting guests first.

SERVES 6

650ml milk, plus more in the fridge...
150ml double cream
1 Scotch bonnet chilli, cut in half
100g dark chocolate, chopped

Pour the milk and cream into a saucepan with the chilli and bring to a simmer. Once the milk is at its optimum heat – and I don't mean temperature! – remove the Scotch bonnet and whisk in the chocolate until the mix is silky-smooth.

Poor into mugs and maybe keep a glass of cold milk on standby in case things get hairy!

PORK BELLY BAPS
WITH POACHED RHUBARB

1kg pork belly, de-boned and
    skin scored
1 tbsp cider vinegar
vegetable oil, for roasting
    and frying
100g mayonnaise (see page 139
    for homemade)
1 tsp smoked paprika
squeeze of lemon juice
8 brioche baps, cut in half
mixed salad leaves
sea salt

For the poached rhubarb
200ml cloudy cider
50g brown sugar
1 cinnamon stick
4 sticks rhubarb, trimmed and
    cut into finger-length sticks

It's brisk in the tent when the heaters aren't roaring. Spring might be in sight, but we can still see our breath in the cold morning air. The tent fills with artists from many different countries and origins, waiting to hear about the schedule for the next six months from our director Cal McCrystal. We need to suppress the cold and unfamiliarity with something special to kick-start the season.

Preheat the oven to 220°C.

Place the pork in a deep saucepan, cover with water and add a couple of pinches of salt. Bring to the boil and cook for 15 minutes, then remove and pat dry with kitchen paper. Transfer to a roasting tray and add the vinegar and a good drizzle of vegetable oil. Sprinkle a good pinch of sea salt over, then rub everything into the scored skin. Roast for 30–45 minutes, keeping an eye on it, until the skin is uniformly golden and crisp and the roasting juices run clear when you pierce the meat with a sharp knife. Remove from the oven and leave to cool.

For the poached rhubarb, bring the cider, brown sugar and cinnamon stick to the boil in a non-reactive saucepan. Turn down the heat to low, drop in the rhubarb and poach for 10 minutes, or until tender but not falling apart. Leave to cool.

When you're ready to eat, mix the mayonnaise with the paprika and lemon juice in a small bowl. Slice the pork belly into 1cm thick slices that will fit into the baps and fry in a skillet or heavy-based frying pan with a very small amount of vegetable oil on a medium heat until crisp. Fill each bap with a slice or two of pork belly, a few sticks of poached rhubarb, a small handful of salad leaves and a good drizzle of the smoky mayo.

linguine

WITH WILD GARLIC AND PUMPKIN-SEED PESTO

SERVES 6

2 handfuls of wild garlic, washed
50g pumpkin seeds
100ml rapeseed oil
50ml olive oil
75g Parmesan
1 packet of dried linguine
    (approx. 500g)
sea salt and black pepper

The hills around Fennells Farm are famous for wild garlic. The scent wafts up from the woods, encouraging you to grab some bags and your walking boots. Ensure you pick the younger leaves as the larger, older ones tend to be slightly more bitter – just follow your nose!

Wash any dirt, twigs, grass and insects from the wild garlic and drain in a colander or salad spinner. Toast the pumpkin seeds in a dry frying pan until they start to pop and do backflips, then remove from the pan and leave to cool.

To make the wild garlic and pumpkin-seed pesto, blanch two-thirds of the wild garlic by dunking it in a saucepan of boiling water for about 30 seconds, then tip into a colander and refresh under the cold tap. Use your hands to squeeze out as much water as possible, then put into a food processor with the rapeseed and olive oils. Blend well, then add all except a handful of the pumpkin seeds (saving some for serving later) and blitz briefly, leaving them slightly coarse, for some texture. Stir through half of the grated Parmesan and season well with salt and pepper.

Bring a large saucepan of salted water to the boil, add the linguine and cook until al dente. Drop in the rest of the wild garlic and let it wilt for 30 seconds, then tip the lot into a colander and drain well. Pour everything back into the saucepan, mix in the pesto, then serve with the reserved pumpkin seeds and the remaining Parmesan.

CIDER WITH ROSIE

MAKES 4 GENEROUS GLASSES

4 cinnamon sticks
660ml still cider
4 x 25ml shots cider brandy
    or Calvados
330ml cloudy apple juice
50g soft brown sugar
1 apple, sliced

Even in the midst of rehearsals, there is always the chance to go for a little jolly after lunch. An entourage of scenic painters, sign writers, prop builders and seamstresses gathers for an adventure through woods filled with wild garlic and fields of cows, and over to Swifts Hill. One of the most iconic spots in the valley, with the Woolpack in Slad down the hill, this is serious *Cider with Rosie* country and the perfect place for an outdoor cocktail.

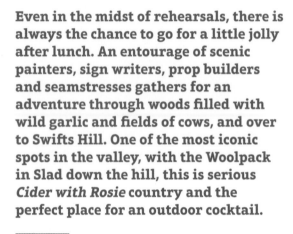

———————

Lightly toast the cinnamon sticks in a dry frying pan.

Pour the cider, cider brandy and apple juice into a large jug, then stir in the sugar and mix everything together well.

Serve in glasses (we like mismatched charity-shop finds) with slices of apple, and the cinnamon sticks for stirring and to give the drink a delicate hint of cinnamon. Careful on the walk back...

TOAD in the HOLE

SERVES 6

12 chipolatas
lard or vegetable oil, for frying
    and greasing
a few sprigs of thyme
English mustard, to serve

**For the Yorkshire pudding
    batter**
2 eggs
150ml whole milk
115g plain flour
pinch of salt
a grating of nutmeg

For the onion gravy
a knob of butter
1 red onion, thinly sliced
    (plus extra to accompany the
    batter, if you like)
1 garlic clove, sliced
1 tsp brown sugar
2 tsp plain flour
250ml warm beef stock
1 tsp Marmite or Bovril
sea salt and black pepper

A British classic and perfect for a cold spring afternoon. We make these in muffin trays to give them a bit more personality and to stop people fighting over how much they get! Of course you have to have a nostalgic gravy with it – thick with onions and plenty of thyme.

For the Yorkshire pudding batter, lightly beat the eggs and milk together with a whisk, then slowly mix into the flour, salt and nutmeg until you have a smooth batter. Leave in the fridge to settle for 30 minutes before using.

Preheat the oven to 220°C.

Lightly brown the chipolatas in a frying pan with a knob of lard or splash of vegetable oil, then remove and set aside.

Pop a small knob of lard or a few drops of oil into each hole of a 12-hole Yorkshire pudding or muffin tray, then heat in the oven for 3–4 minutes. When the chipolatas are cool enough to handle, cut them into 4cm lengths. Remove the batter from the fridge and give it a quick stir. Remove the hot tray from the oven and divide your par-cooked chipolatas and the thyme evenly between the holes, adding a sprig of thyme per hole and some raw red onion if you like, then pour in the batter. Return the tray to the oven and do not open the oven for 20–30 minutes.

Meanwhile, for the gravy, melt the butter in the same frying pan you used for the chipolatas, then add the onion and garlic. Sweat down over low heat until soft, then add the brown sugar. Once the onion has become almost translucent, sprinkle in the flour and cook, stirring, for 2–3 minutes. Slowly add the beef stock and Marmite or Bovril, stirring frequently as the gravy starts to thicken. Bring to the boil, then season to taste, chuck in another few sprigs of thyme simply ripped up with your hands, and keep warm until needed.

When the toad in the holes are golden and firm, they are ready to serve – with a good helping of gravy and a dollop of fiery English mustard.

Cal's Tea Party

The way to our wonderful director's
heart is a slice of cake and a cuppa.
The madness of rehearsals requires
a tea party of Earl Grey tea, grapefruit
meringue pies and a stack of chocolate
brownies to inspire even more creative
thought. It's never long before he's
joined by a few friends...

*NOT FOR THE
FAINT-HEARTED

THE STRONGMAN CAKE

THIS STRONGMAN CAKE IS CHALLENGE ENOUGH FOR ANYONE -- THE MORE RUM, THE BETTER!

SERVES 12, OR 1 STRONGMAN

400g soft unsalted butter
400g caster sugar
8 large eggs
360g self-raising flour
4 tsp baking powder
60g cocoa powder, plus extra
  for dusting
100g preserved ginger, grated
grated zest of 2 limes
pinch of salt

For the filling and icing
500g mascarpone
150g dark brown sugar
2 x 25ml shots dark rum
juice of 2 limes

Preheat the oven to 170°C and line 2 × 20cm springform cake tins with baking parchment.

In an electric mixer fitted with the flat beater attachment or in a food processor, cream the butter and sugar until white and fluffy. Add the eggs, one by one, while still mixing. Add the rest of the ingredients and mix to a smooth batter. Divide the batter evenly between the two tins and bake for 30 minutes, or until the tip of a skewer inserted into the centre comes out clean. Carefully remove the cakes from the tins and leave to cool on a rack.

To make the filling and icing, wash and dry the mixer and fit it with the whisk attachment. Add the mascarpone, sugar, rum, lime juice and mix well until you have a glossy and smooth icing.

Using a serrated knife, trim and slice each cake in half horizontally so you end up with four identical, level sections. Begin building the tower of cake, smothering each layer with the filling to hold them in place, then cover the whole structure with most of the remaining icing, smoothing the surface with a palette knife dipped in hot water. Spoon the rest of the icing into a piping bag and squeeze out some intimidating peaks. Dust with cocoa powder and there we have it!

LEMON, LAPSANG AND LAVENDER CAKE

SERVES 8

50g poppy seeds
225g soft unsalted butter
225g caster sugar
225g self-raising flour
2½ tsp baking powder
4 large eggs
finely grated zest of 3 lemons
pinch of salt

For the syrup
juice of 3 lemons
1 lapsang souchong tea bag
200g icing sugar
20g dried or fresh (unsprayed)
  lavender flowers

Tea cake at its best – this is another easy cake that can be made in a food processor. The lapsang souchong tea adds a brilliant smoky flavour.

Preheat the oven to 160°C and line a loaf tin about 30 × 11 x 7cm deep with baking parchment.

Lightly toast the poppy seeds in a dry frying pan for a minute or so, just until they smell nutty. In a stand mixer fitted with the flat beater attachment or in a food processor, cream the butter and sugar until white and fluffy. Add the rest of the ingredients and mix to a smooth batter. Pour the batter into the tin and bake for 30–35 minutes, until a skewer inserted into the centre of the cake comes out clean.

Meanwhile, for the syrup, put the lemon juice in a small saucepan with 2 tablespoons water, add the tea bag and simmer over low heat for a few minutes to infuse. Remove the tea bags, then stir in the icing sugar and lavender. Use a fork to stab holes all over the hot lemon cake, then pour the syrup over the top. Remove from the tin and leave to cool on a wire rack before carving a generous slice to enjoy with a brew from an over-sized teapot…

FLAPJACKS WITH TOASTED SEEDS

SERVES 8

100g mixed seeds
250g unsalted butter
175g golden syrup
175g muscovado sugar
300g jumbo oats
100g raisins
1 tsp ground ginger
1 tsp ground cinnamon
pinch of salt

This treat is soft, chewy and delicious. We add seeds and dried fruit to give the illusion of it being healthy… but it's not!

Preheat the oven to 170°C and line a deep baking tray, 20 x 30cm, with baking parchment.

Lightly toast the seeds in a dry frying pan, just until they smell nutty, then remove from the pan and leave to cool.

Put the butter, golden syrup and sugar in a large, heavy-based saucepan and melt over medium heat. Add the seeds, oats, raisins, ginger, cinnamon and salt and mix well.

Scrape the mixture into the baking tray, pressing it down firmly and evenly. Bake for 30 minutes until ever so slightly browned on top but still soft.

Leave to cool in the tray, then cut into chunky squares.

SCRUMPY APPLE AND BRAMBLE TART WITH HAZELNUT CRUMBLE

Put your Sunday roast on in the morning, then take the dogs for a walk through the orchards and fill a bag with apples and blackberries. Open your door to the comforting smell of the roast, light the fire, put the roasties in the oven, pop the apples on to stew with the blackberries and enjoy the wonders of Sunday. Just make sure it's OK to scrump before you inadvertently break the law!

SERVES 8

3 cooking apples
250g blackberries
100ml scrumpy cider
125g caster sugar
squeeze of lemon juice
1 cinnamon stick
175g unsalted butter
250g plain flour
125g light brown sugar
50g crushed hazelnuts
50g rolled oats

For the shortcrust pastry
300g plain flour, plus extra
    for dusting
140g unsalted butter
90g caster sugar
4 egg yolks
pinch of salt

For the shortcrust pastry, put the flour, butter, sugar and egg yolks in a food processor and pulse until incorporated. Turn out onto a lightly floured surface and knead for 2–3 minutes until you have a smooth dough. Wrap in clingfilm and rest in the fridge for at least 30 minutes.

Preheat the oven to 170°C and lightly grease a 25cm fluted tart tin.

On a lightly floured surface, roll out the pastry into a large circle, 2–3mm thick, and use it to line the tart tin, using your fingers to gently press it down into the corners. Roll the rolling pin over the top of the case to remove any excess pastry. Prick the base with a fork. Return to the fridge for 10 minutes to rest once more.

Line the chilled pastry case with baking parchment and fill with baking beans. Blind-bake for 15 minutes, then remove the beans and parchment and bake for a further 10 minutes until the base has slightly browned.

After a forage in the orchards and hedgerows (or the supermarket), peel, core and roughly dice your apples. Pick out any leaves, stalks or bugs from the blackberries and rinse under the tap in a colander. Pour the scrumpy into a heavy-based saucepan and simmer until reduced by half. Add the caster sugar, lemon juice, cinnamon stick, 100g of the butter and the apples. Cook for about 15 minutes until the fruit begins to break down but some of it is still intact. Remove from the heat and gently stir in the blackberries, then set aside.

Combine the flour and brown sugar in a bowl, then rub in the remaining 75g butter until the mixture resembles fine breadcrumbs. Stir in the hazelnuts and oats and spread out on a baking tray. Bake until crisp, golden brown and vaguely holding its shape – a little like a cracked pavement. Break up with a spoon and bake for another 5–10 minutes until even more golden and visibly crunchy.

Fill the tart shell with the fruit mix, leaving some room for the crumble topping. Break up the crumble and sprinkle over the tart, covering the fruit. Bake for 10–15 minutes until the mix has warmed through. Serve, ideally in front of an open fire...

GRAPEFRUIT MERINGUE PIES

½ quantity of Shortcrust Pastry
(page 45)

For the grapefruit curd
finely grated zest and juice of
3 yellow grapefruit to make
350ml of juice
100g caster sugar
40g cornflour
100g chilled unsalted butter,
cut into small cubes
1 whole egg, plus 3 yolks,
lightly beaten
5–6 lemon verbena leaves,
finely chopped (if you can
find them)

For the meringue
130g caster sugar
squeeze of lemon juice
4 egg whites, at room
temperature
½ tsp cream of tartar

Preheat the oven to 170°C and lightly grease the holes of a muffin tray.

On a lightly floured surface, roll out the pastry until 2–3mm thick and stamp out 9 rounds using a large scone or cookie cutter to fit the holes of the muffin tray. Line 9 holes with the pastry rounds and chill in the fridge for 10 minutes.

Line the chilled pastry cases with baking parchment and fill with baking beans. Blind-bake for 10 minutes, then remove the beans and parchment and bake for a further 5 minutes until the bases have slightly browned.

For the grapefruit curd, put the grapefruit zest and juice into a non-reactive saucepan, add the sugar and cornflour and whisk to combine. Bring to the boil, stirring constantly. The mix should begin to thicken – once it has, remove from the heat and add the butter, a little at a time, stirring well until the butter is incorporated. Stir in the egg and yolks, put back over low heat and return to a simmer. Stir until the curd really thickens, then pass through a sieve into a bowl. Stir through the lemon verbena, if using, then fill the pastry cases with the curd.

Turn up the oven to 210°C for browning the meringue toppings (unless you're going to use a blowtorch instead).

For the meringue, put the caster sugar into a saucepan with 100ml water and a squeeze of lemon juice to stop the sugar crystallising. Place over medium heat and bring to 121°C, using a cooking thermometer.

Use an electric mixer to whisk the egg whites with the cream of tartar until soft peaks form. With the mixer running slowly, start adding the hot sugar syrup – the meringue should puff up and stiffen like marshmallow. When all the sugar syrup has been incorporated, keep whisking until the meringue has cooled to room temperature. Scrape the meringue into a piping bag fitted with a plain nozzle and pipe – or, more simply, spoon – over the pies.

Either bake for 10 minutes or blast the meringue toppings with a blowtorch until golden. Serve warm.

At breakfast I'd always go for a pink grapefruit, and the yellow ones can sometimes get overlooked unless you like things bitter… But its sharpness works so well in a meringue pie, ideally with a touch of lemon verbena mixed through the curd if you want to be fancy. You'll need a sugar thermometer to make the meringue, and then you can either bake it or quickly glaze it with a blowtorch, if you have one. I also like to make this pie with blood orange or Seville orange curd.

CHOCOLATE BROWNIES

A TRIP TO GIFFORDS ISN'T THE SAME WITHOUT ONE

MAKES 6–8 PORTIONS

225g unsalted butter
225g dark chocolate, broken
   into pieces
350g caster sugar
4 large eggs
pinch of salt
175g plain flour

Consider this just a base to which you can add numerous other ingredients to make things more interesting, such as glacé or fresh cherries, mint, white chocolate, coffee, vanilla, Maltesers, anything you like! Do what you will with your brownies – just don't ever overcook them. There's quite simply nothing worse than a dry brownie, as Lil Rice will tell you!

Preheat the oven to 180°C and line a 30 × 20cm brownie tin with baking parchment.

In a saucepan, melt the butter and bring almost to boiling point before removing from the heat and whisking in the chocolate until smooth. The residual heat from the butter should be enough to melt the chocolate but if not, scrape the mixture into a non-metallic bowl and pop it into the microwave for a few seconds.

In a large mixing bowl, beat the sugar and eggs with a pinch of salt until light and fluffy – this is easier in a stand mixer. Slowly add the melted chocolate and butter and keep mixing until fully incorporated. Sift in the flour and gently fold into the batter.

Pour the batter into the tin and bake for 20–30 minutes, depending on how set you want your brownies – but make sure there's still a wobble in the centre, so you get a nice smooth texture with no graininess.

Turn out onto a wire rack and leave to cool a little before cutting into 6 pieces.

PRESERVES AT FENNELLS FARM

Rehearsals provide a brilliant opportunity to start making bits for the coming season. The mason jars reappear from storage and we get on with filling them with pickled veg, chutneys, jams and salts. It's a brilliant feeling popping open a jar and releasing the tastes and smells that capture the feeling of when it was made.

PICKLED VEGETABLES

Don't blame us if you find yourself standing in front of the fridge after midnight, with your hand stuck in the jar, prising out the last vegetables from the bottom. They're strangely addictive.

MAKES 1 LARGE JAR

750g mixed vegetables, washed and trimmed
2 bay leaves
250ml white wine vinegar
30g caster sugar
2 tsp salt
1 tsp coriander seeds
1 tsp fennel seeds
3 garlic cloves

Run a 1-litre Kilner jar (or several smaller jars) through a dishwasher to sterilise.

Slice any larger vegetables nice and small before packing them into the sterilised Kilner jar with the bay leaves.

Put the rest of the ingredients into a non-reactive saucepan with 250ml water and bring to the boil. Remove from the heat, let cool slightly, then pour into the jar to cover the veg and seal the lid.

These will keep, unopened, for 5–6 months and once opened, will keep in the fridge for up to a week.

PICCALILLI

Pantry fodder. A brilliant condiment to have in the store-cupboard, or out in pride of place, showcasing what you've grown on your allotment.

MAKES 2 LARGE JARS

1kg vegetables – allotment raid! (e.g. green
    beans, cucumbers, radishes, cauliflower,
    sprouting broccoli, spring onions), trimmed
70g sea salt
15g yellow mustard seeds
1 tsp crushed cumin seeds
1 tsp crushed coriander seeds
50g cornflour
800ml cider vinegar
300g caster sugar
5 bay leaves
2 star anise
2 tbsp English mustard powder
1 tbsp ground turmeric

Cut the veg into small pieces, mix with the salt and leave in a sealed container in the fridge for a day.

Next day, run 2 × 1-litre Kilner jars through a dishwasher to sterilise. Toast the mustard seeds and crushed cumin and coriander seeds in a dry frying pan until they start to smoke slightly. In a small bowl, mix the cornflour with a splash of the vinegar until smooth.

Put the remaining vinegar, sugar, bay leaves and all the spices into a stainless-steel saucepan and bring to the boil. Add the cornflour mix and cook, stirring, for 5 minutes until thick, then leave to cool.

Wash the salt off the veg thoroughly, then add to the cooled piccalilli sauce, mixing well. Transfer to the sterilised Kilner jars and seal.

This will keep, unopened, for 5–6 months and once opened, will keep in the fridge for up to a week.

CELERY SALT

When it's time to harvest the celery and celeriac from the allotment, the leaves generally fall victim to the compost heap; however, this is a wonderful way to make use of them.

MAKES 1 SMALL JAR

1 small bunch celery leaves
1 small bunch celeriac leaves
50g fine salt
50g flaky sea salt
50g pink Himalayan salt

Run a 100-ml Kilner jar through a dishwasher to sterilise and dry thoroughly.

Pick the leaves from the stalks, then pop them on a plate and microwave for 3 minutes at a time, giving the leaves a mix around every time. Keep going until the leaves are completely dried and crumbly – this takes longer than you think.

Leave to cool completely before blending them together in a food processor with all three salts until the leaves are combined. Transfer to the sterilised Kilner jar and seal.

This will keep at room temperature for up to 6 months.

CHILLI OIL

On request, we add this to our pizzas to give them a good kick! Use chillies that are as hot or as mild as you like.

MAKES 1 LITRE

1 whole garlic bulb
4 red chillies, sliced lengthways
1 litre olive oil
3 sprigs of rosemary
1 tsp smoked paprika

Run a 1-litre bottle through a dishwasher to sterilise.

Separate the garlic bulb into cloves and place on a board with the chillies, then crush with the base of a heavy saucepan. Pop the crushed garlic and chillies into the saucepan, along with the olive oil, rosemary and paprika. Place over low heat and simmer gently for 20 minutes.

Pour the oil into the sterilised bottle and seal.

This will keep in the fridge for up to 6 months.

HOLLANDAISE VINEGAR

This flavoured vinegar is not just for making Hollandaise Sauce (page 224) – it's also marvellous for adding to any sauces and dressings that need to be a bit sharper. To make béarnaise vinegar, add a small handful of tarragon stalks to the Kilner jar before sealing.

MAKES 500ML

400ml white wine vinegar
100ml white wine
3 shallots, thinly sliced
2 garlic cloves, simply crushed
    with the back of a knife
10 black peppercorns
2 bay leaves

Run a 500-ml Kilner jar through a dishwasher to sterilise.

Put all the ingredients in a stainless-steel saucepan and simmer for 20 minutes. Pour into the sterilised jar and seal.

This will keep, unopened, for 5–6 months and once opened, will keep in the fridge for up to a week.

RED CABBAGE SAUERKRAUT

A little bit different from the norm, but the beautiful colour makes you want to pop the lid as soon as you see it.

MAKES 1 LARGE JAR

1kg red cabbage
40g sea salt
1 tsp caraway seeds
8–10 juniper berries

Slice the cabbage nice and thinly using a mandoline or food processor and put into a deep plastic tub or a glass/ceramic crock.

Put the salt into a small saucepan with a splash of water and place over medium heat, stirring to dissolve the salt. Take off the heat, then pour in 1 litre fresh water to make a brine.

Mix the caraway seeds and juniper berries into the cabbage, then pour in the brine. Cover the cabbage with a plate topped with a tin can, for example, to keep it submerged under the brine. Leave at room temperature for 3–4 days, until you see soft bubbles emerging.

Run a 1-litre Kilner jar through a dishwasher to sterilise. Transfer the sauerkraut to the sterilised jar, seal and store for at least 5 days for optimum sourness and you're ready!

This will keep, unopened, for up to 5 months and once opened, will keep in the fridge for up to a week.

PRESERVED GINGER

Perfect for when you have a dessert that needs a kick – or slice thinly and roll in granulated sugar for a fiery treat.

MAKES 1 LARGE JAR

500g ginger
500g granulated sugar

Run a 1-litre Kilner jar through a dishwasher to sterilise.

Peel the ginger and cut into 3-cm chunks, then put into a saucepan and cover with water. Bring to the boil and let it bubble away for 40 minutes, then strain out the ginger and discard the water.

Put the sugar into the saucepan with 500ml fresh water and bring to a simmer. Return the ginger to the pan and simmer for 20–30 minutes until the ginger starts to go slightly translucent.

Carefully transfer to the sterilised jar, ensuring the ginger is completely covered in liquid, and seal.

This will keep, unopened, for up to 6 months and once opened, will keep in the fridge for up to a week.

GREEN TABASCO

Salty, hot and tart, this is one of the most incredible condiments I can think of. It also has the most wonderfully inviting look to it on the shelf.

MAKES 1 SMALL BOTTLE

200ml white wine vinegar
2 tsp salt
1 garlic clove, crushed
100g green jalapeño peppers,
    deseeded and thinly sliced

Run a 330-ml bottle through a dishwasher to sterilise.

Put the vinegar, salt and garlic into a stainless-steel saucepan and bring to the boil. Add the peppers, then take off the heat and leave to macerate for 10 minutes. Transfer to a food processor and blend until smooth. Transfer to the sterilised bottle and seal.

This will keep, unopened, for up to 2 months and once opened, will keep in the fridge for up to a week.

CHAPTER TWO

LET THE PLAY BEGIN

As theatre directors say, a show is never finished, it is just abandoned. The whole company gets nervous as opening night approaches: nervous because the show will be in front of the public, and nervous because the work of the creative team will soon be over and, like children leaving home, we will soon be on the road on our own.

It is a thrilling transition from the relative privacy of rehearsals to opening the gate of the car park field, putting out the cushions in the tent, warming up the candy-floss machine and welcoming the public into our world. The restaurant moves from the barn to the front field, and prepares for service. This is the first time the restaurant crew will pack up and move the restaurant and, just as the technicians iron out a hundred minute problems in the tent, so the restaurant team figure out how they are going to make sure that every element of the restaurant can be packed and re-packed during the summer ahead. The circus has a hundred thousand moving parts, and almost no element of it is a repeated or identical process. It is an accountant's nightmare. But this is also what makes Giffords Circus so lovely: it is a miniature village or, in a way, a miniature city – cosmopolitan and organic, multi-layered and mysterious, with elements of internal competition, politics, unwritten rules and boundaries, a promise of late nights, transgression and fun.

Despite numerous rehearsals, there is nothing quite like that opening-night feeling. Nerves have to be breathed through and churning stomachs settled. Ols and his team prepare a hot toddy before the first show. The café wagon is opened and the coffee machine is primed to serve a special mocha to the front of house. The days are long, but the weather is unpredictable and the evenings can be freezing – performers in sequins, fishnets and dainty shoes await their call in giant puffer overcoats under the light of hundreds of festoon bulbs. Everything at that moment is strange and new and thrilling. Nerves keep rising as the first house fills and the rumours start…

'Gerry from Wookey is here with 20 people!"
'There are four theatre critics in the front row!"
'My mum is here!"
'My eyelash is stuck."
'Johnny Flynn is here."

DESPITE NUMEROUS REHEARSALS, THERE IS NOTHING QUITE LIKE THAT OPENING-NIGHT FEELING. NERVES HAVE TO BE BREATHED THROUGH AND CHURNING STOMACHS SETTLED. OLS AND HIS TEAM PREPARE A HOT TODDY BEFORE THE FIRST SHOW.

We stick to the back tent and try to compose ourselves. I know that, just before a show, I cannot speak to anyone outside of the company. We all concentrate on controlling our nerves and focusing on the performance ahead.

Likewise, in the restaurant, the chefs must make the transition from cooking solely for the company to feeding the public. For the last three weeks, every day they have made three hot meals for one hundred people. But this marks the start of the feasting and hospitality, and Ols is cooking up a storm. Everyone in the Big Top is served lamb roasted over the fire, with mint chimichurri and stewed beans – the first of many feasts for a circus-going public. This is celebration cooking, rich and sumptuous food for opening night. Our larder is English, and our ingredients are local and seasonal, yet the kitchen has just a hint of Napoleonic canteen about it – a *grande bouffe* for an army set on feasting over fighting, savouring morale-boosting food from the fat of the land.

WELCOME PARTY AT FENNELLS FARM

With the opening night approaching, we need something special to feed to everyone after the very first show. It has to be eye-catching and create excitement. The smell from the lamb asado will get people going – all sizzling meat and wood smoke. The bar is being set up, kegs are being knocked in and prosecco corks are starting to pop. The first of many, many people start to trickle into the front of house looking to be entertained, amazed and amused.

PRE-SHOW HOT TODDY

A hot toddy is usually drunk when you are sniffly or cold, but it's also great for nerves – just don't have too many before attempting the trapeze…

Put all the ingredients apart from the whisky into a saucepan and simmer for 5 minutes, adding the booze at the end, so none of the alcohol steams off!

Pour into goblets and take a few minutes to enjoy the aroma, then go for it!

SERVES 4

400ml boiling water
100g clear honey
25g chunk of ginger
4 cloves
2 cinnamon sticks
5 x 25ml shots of whisky

LAMB ASADO
WITH MINT CHIMICHURRI AND STEWED BEANS

SERVES 8

2kg lamb shoulder, butterflied
olive oil
sea salt and black pepper

For the stewed beans
300g pork sausage or chorizo
500g pork ribs/ears/tail
1 smoked ham hock
1 onion, diced
2 garlic cloves, thinly sliced
5 sprigs of thyme
2 bay leaves
600g white beans, soaked
     overnight

For the mint chimichurri
2 bunches of mint
200ml white wine vinegar
30g brown sugar
2 tsp ground white pepper
1 green chilli
1 tsp salt

With at least a hundred hungry mouths to feed at the opening-night party, it's time to fire up the asado grill we've dug in Nell's back garden. Lamb with mint sauce has a special place in our hearts and this Latin American-inspired version makes a perfect start to the season. We buy whole lambs from the local butcher and let them slowly cook over the fire pit for several hours, but a lamb shoulder works brilliantly on a smaller scale.

Once the fire is burning, get the stewed beans on the go. Brown the sausage, pork and ham hock in a large saucepan with a little oil, then remove from the pan and set aside. Add the onion and garlic to the same pan, along with the thyme and bay leaves, and let them sweat and soften for a few minutes before adding the drained beans. Return the browned meats to the pan and pour in enough water to cover. Bring to the boil, partly cover the pan, then leave to stew over low heat for 2 hours.

Meanwhile, with the grill embers stoked, rub the lamb all over with olive oil, salt and pepper, then place on an asado spike if you have one, but a wire rack works just as well. Sit above the roaring fire 2 feet away from the embers, or in the oven, and cook for about 2 hours, turning every so often to cook evenly, until the meat becomes tender. Leave to rest for 15–20 minutes before you carve.

Alternatively, you can use a griddle pan at home to sear the meat over a high heat and get that wonderful charred flavour before transferring it to an oven, preheated to 180°C, for about 2 hours for well done or 1½ hours for medium.

When the lamb is nearly ready, pop all the ingredients for the mint chimichurri into a blender and whizz until almost smooth, then transfer to a bowl. (Don't be tempted to make this too far ahead, or the vinegar will turn the mint a dull brown colour.)

Slice the lamb and serve with the mint chimichurri and the stewed beans. What a way to kick-start the season!

POUSSINS

ROASTED IN BEER, HONEY, THYME AND BUTTER

Poussins, or French hens, are slightly sweet and can take on a lot of flavour. You can roast them whole, or in half, but here it works best if they are spatchcocked. Ask your butcher to do this – or send a knife down either side of the spine, remove it, then take out the wishbone and any other cartilage and flatten the birds. This recipe has bitterness from the beer, sweetness from the honey, richness from the butter and aromatic flavour from the thyme.

SERVES 4

50ml red wine vinegar
100ml honey
2 star anise
2 bay leaves
1 bunch of thyme
4 poussins, spatchcocked
olive oil, for frying
1 whole garlic bulb, cut in half
   across the equator
100g soft butter
330ml golden ale
500ml chicken stock
sea salt and black pepper
Hasselback Potatoes (page 78)
   and Red Cabbage Sauerkraut
   (page 60), warmed through
   in a parchment parcel in the
   oven, to serve

Put the vinegar, honey, star anise, bay leaves and half of the thyme in a frying pan over high heat and bring to the boil, stirring well. Pour the liquid over the poussins in a couple of large dishes and leave to marinate in the fridge for as long as possible – ideally overnight.

Preheat the oven to 200°C.

Lift the poussins out of the marinade, reserving it for later, and pat them dry. Season well with salt and pepper. Get a frying pan nice and hot over medium–high heat, add a drizzle of olive oil and lower in the poussins with a satisfying sizzle. Once they have taken on a nice golden colour, place the garlic bulb halves, cut side up in a roasting tray and perch the poussins on top. Smear the soft butter over the poussins, then scatter over the remaining thyme and roast the poussins for about 20–25 minutes until the birds are firm to the touch and the roasting juices run clear when you pierce the meat with a sharp knife.

Move the poussins to a wire rack to rest and put the roasting tray on the stove over medium heat. Pour the reserved marinade into the tin and cook for 5–10 minutes until reduced to a syrup. Pour in the golden ale and cook again until it bubbles and has reduced slightly more. Finally, add the stock and reduce a little further to make a delicious jus.

Serve the poussins with the jus, roasted garlic, Hasselback Potatoes and the Red Cabbage Sauerkraut.

Hasselback Potatoes

SERVES 6

about 12 waxy potatoes, washed
100g soft butter or beef
 dripping
sea salt and black pepper

These are the perfect accompaniment for the poussins on the previous page. Swedish in origin and usually topped with breadcrumbs or ground almonds, these crunchy potatoes are best – in our view – plain and simple, with just a bit of salt and pepper, and some dripping or butter.

Preheat the oven to 160°C.

Don't peel the potatoes – these are far tastier with the earthy flavour of their skins.

Slice down through the potato every couple of millimetres but without going all the way through – we place each potato on the benchtop, nestled between 2 chopping boards, to stop the knife going too deep.

Place the potatoes on a baking tray, smother with the butter or dripping and season well with salt and pepper. Bake for 30–40 minutes, until the ridges are wonderfully crisp and golden.

Root Vegetable Gratin

SERVES 8–10

750ml double cream
250ml milk
3 garlic cloves, bashed with the
    flat of a knife
3 sprigs of thyme
3 large starchy potatoes
2 beetroots
2 parsnips
½ swede
½ celeriac
200g gruyère cheese, grated
a grating of nutmeg
sea salt and white pepper

We've had this on the menu so many times, and people love it so much that they try to recreate it at home – but sometimes with disastrous results if they leave out the potatoes. It's the starch that holds it together, so it's imperative to include them... and the rest of what you use can be whatever you dig out of the allotment!

In a saucepan, bring the cream, milk, garlic and thyme to a simmer. Remove from the heat, cover and leave to infuse for 30 minutes or so.

Meanwhile, peel the potatoes and root vegetables, then cut into 2–3mm-thick slices, ideally using a mandoline.

Pass the infused cream through a sieve and season well with salt and pepper.

Preheat the oven to 160°C.

In a deep baking dish, start layering your gratin: a neat layer of potatoes and roots, followed by some of the cream, cheese, nutmeg, salt and pepper. Do this several times until you run out of vegetables – make sure there are potatoes in each layer and finish the top with plenty of cheese.

Bake for 30–40 minutes, depending on how deep the gratin is – prod it with a knife to make sure it's cooked all the way through. Serve, still bubbling, on the table and let your guests dig in!

NETTLE SOUP

SERVES 6

knob of butter
1 onion, diced
2 celery sticks, diced
3 garlic cloves, thinly sliced
2 bay leaves
2 large potatoes, peeled and
    sliced
1½ litres vegetable stock
1 handful of spinach
3–4 handfuls of young nettles,
    well washed
sea salt and white pepper
vegetable oil, for deep-frying
crème fraîche, toasted seeds
    and Penny Buns (page 136),
    to serve (optional)

Nettles have a flavour that's almost indescribable – rich, but also sour and fresh – which is perhaps why I like them so much. Also, I can't think of an ingredient we find in such abundance wherever we pitch up. Needless to say, wear gloves when foraging for them... Another thing that's very important is to pick the leaves early on in the year when they're young, as older leaves can have a laxative effect! The soup goes rather well with Penny Buns.

Melt the butter in a large saucepan, add the onion, celery, garlic and bay leaves and sweat them down for a few minutes. Add the potatoes and stock and simmer for 30 minutes until the potatoes are cooked through. Add the spinach and most of the nettles (saving a handful for deep frying later), then return the soup to the boil and remove from the heat. Allow to cool for a few minutes before transferring to a blender. Whizz the soup until smooth, and season with salt and pepper to taste.

Pour a couple of centimetres of vegetable oil into a small, heavy-based saucepan over medium heat. Heat the oil until a cube of bread dropped into it turns golden in about 15 seconds (about 180°C on a cooking thermometer). Now deep-fry the reserved nettle leaves just until they are dark green and crisp, being careful to shield your eyes as the oil can spit with some ferocity. Drain on kitchen paper, then drop into the soup with a drizzle of crème fraîche and some toasted seeds. Serve with Penny Buns, if you like.

HEAD, HOCK AND TROTTER TERRINE
WITH DUCK-EGG SAUCE

SERVES 8–10

1 large onion, peeled
2 carrots, peeled
2 celery sticks
2 leeks, well washed
2 smoked ham hocks
1 pig's head
2 trotters
2 garlic cloves, peeled
2 bay leaves
5 black peppercorns
4 cloves
3 star anise
pickled carrots (use the recipe
   on page 53), bunch of
   watercress and slices of grilled
   sourdough, to serve

For the duck-egg sauce
3 egg yolks
1 tbsp cider vinegar
1 tbsp English mustard
300ml rapeseed oil
3 hard-boiled duck eggs
squeeze of lemon juice
1 banana shallot, finely chopped
50g Lilliput capers, finely
   chopped
handful of parsley, finely
   chopped
sea salt and white pepper

We have been fans of Fergus Henderson for a long time, and his nose-to-tail philosophy really works for us. We get whole pigs from Toti Gifford's farm, which are wonderful, but managing to put every cut on the menu can be difficult, so a lot of them go into a terrine. This one works wonderfully, and if you live on a farm surrounded by rapeseed fields and an orchard, with a flour mill nearby, then you can find all the ingredients in the fields around you! Otherwise, your local shops should be able to oblige…

Roughly chop one half of the vegetables (keeping aside the other half) and place in a stockpot or large saucepan with the hocks, head and trotters, garlic, bay leaves, peppercorns, cloves and star anise. Pour in enough water to cover, then bring to the boil and skim off any impurities that rise to the surface. Turn down to a simmer and cook for around 4–5 hours, until the meat starts to fall away from the bones. Drain off the liquor into another pan and simmer until reduced by half. The natural gelatine content will help to set the terrine. When the head, hock and trotters are cool enough to handle, pick off all the meat (discard the fat, skin and gristle) and place in a bowl.

Line a 1.3-litre terrine mould with clingfilm. Now chop the remaining uncooked vegetables finely. Sauté in a little vegetable oil, then mix with the picked meat and the reduced liquor. Spoon into the terrine mould, pressing it down firmly, then leave to set in the fridge for 2–3 hours.

Meanwhile, make the duck-egg sauce. Using a handheld whisk or an electric mixer, whisk together the egg yolks, vinegar and mustard. Whisking constantly, slowly drizzle in the rapeseed oil to make a smooth, mayonnaise-like sauce. Grate the hard-boiled eggs into the sauce through a box grater and also add the lemon juice, shallot, capers and parsley. Season to taste with salt and pepper.

Carefully turn out the terrine onto a chopping board. Using a hot knife, cut slices and serve with a dollop of duck-egg sauce, a few pickled carrots, some watercress and a couple of slices of grilled sourdough. Perfect with a pint of cider!

BRAISED BEEF SHORT RIBS

WITH STICKY DATES AND HAZELNUTS

SERVES 8

2kg beef short ribs as one piece
rapeseed oil, for frying
1 carrot, roughly diced
1 celery stick, roughly diced
1 onion, roughly diced
1 leek, washed and roughly
    diced
1 whole garlic bulb, cut in half
    across the equator
100g tomato purée
1 small bunch of thyme
2 bay leaves
200ml red wine
100ml Port
2 litres beef stock
1 bunch of baby carrots,
    trimmed
4 banana shallots, peeled
    and halved lengthways
100g hazelnuts (or cobnuts)
200g pitted dates
sea salt and black pepper
Root Vegetable Gratin (page
    79), to serve

We all love ribs but these are something else entirely, with more tender meat and a lovely richness coming from the bones. Hazelnuts add a nutty flavour and crunch, as do cobnuts, if they are in season – and if you have the patience to shell them! These work so well with some steamed greens and the Root Vegetable Gratin.

Preheat the oven to 150°C.

Begin by seasoning the ribs well with salt and pepper. Heat a little oil in a heavy-based frying pan or skillet and use to brown the ribs. When they're nice and brown all over, lay them in a deep roasting tray. Add the carrot, celery, onion, leek and garlic to the frying pan and cook, stirring, until golden brown around the edges. Stir in the tomato purée, thyme, bay leaves, red wine, port and stock, scraping up any caramelised bits from the pan, then pour into the tin with the ribs. Cover with foil and braise in the oven for 3 hours, or until the meat is tender but hasn't completely disintegrated! Remove the foil and introduce the baby carrots and shallots. Roast, uncovered, for another 30 minutes until the carrots and shallots are cooked.

When the ribs are done, remove the tin from the oven and increase the oven temperature to 180°C. Spread the hazelnuts on a baking tray and toast in the oven for 10 minutes until starting to brown. Crush roughly using a pestle and mortar.

Soak the dates in boiling water for 15 minutes then drain and roughly chop.

Drain the juices from the roasting tray into a saucepan, place over a high heat and simmer until reduced by two-thirds and syrupy. Stir in the dates to make a sticky glaze.

Use a pastry brush to paint the ribs with the glaze, then return to the oven for another 15 minutes with the roasted carrots and shallots. Paint over some more of the sticky glaze and add a good sprinkling of hazelnuts. Serve with the Root Vegetable Gratin on the side.

OXTAIL, SHIN & OYSTER PIE

WITH BEER AND BORAGE

SERVES 6

500g beef shin or any braising
   steak, diced
500g oxtail, cut into 5cm
   chunks
20g plain flour, plus extra for
   dusting
olive oil
1 carrot, diced
1 leek, well washed and diced
3 shallots, diced
2 celery sticks, diced
2 garlic cloves, finely chopped
2 sprigs of thyme
330-ml bottle of Old Hooky or
   any golden ale
4–5 dashes of Worcestershire
   sauce
500ml beef stock
12 oysters, shucked and shells
   reserved
handful of borage leaves,
   chopped
1 quantity Suet Pastry (page
   148), chilled
2 egg yolks, beaten, for egg
   wash
sea salt and black pepper
steamed purple sprouting
   broccoli, to serve

Dredge the beef and oxtail in the flour, then season with salt and pepper. In a cast-iron pot, heat a drizzle of oil over medium–high heat and brown the beef and oxtail. When they're nice and brown all over, remove from the pot and add the carrot, leek, shallots, celery, garlic and thyme, plus a little more oil and a pinch of salt. When everything is nicely softened, return the meat to the pot, along with the ale, Worcestershire sauce and stock. Stir well, then pop a lid on and simmer for 2–3 hours, until the meat is just starting to pull away from the oxtail bone – do not overcook it, or the meat will be dry. Remove the pie filling from the heat and leave to cool slightly, then chill in the fridge for at least an hour. It's very important that everything is cold before you assemble the pie, otherwise the pastry will immediately sink and not cook properly.

Preheat the oven to 190°C and get 6 individual pie dishes ready.

Now it's time to build the pies: cut the oysters in half and stir into the pie filling, along with the borage leaves and a decent amount of salt and pepper.

On a lightly floured surface, roll out the chilled pastry. You want it quite thick, bearing in mind it will rise to almost double its size in the oven – approximately 5mm. Cut out circles big enough to fit over the pie dishes with an overhang of about 3cm all around.

Brush some egg wash around the edge of the pastry to create a seal, then lay over the pies, egg-wash side down, pressing all around the rim of the dish with your fingers to seal. Generously egg wash the tops of the pies before pressing a cleaned oyster shell into the top of each one.

Bake for 20 minutes, or until the pastry is golden, then serve with some purple sprouting broccoli – and a glass of beer!

KNICKER-
BOCKER
GLORY

Any or all of the following:
  chocolate brownies,
  chocolate crème pâtissière,
  whipped mascarpone cream,
  chocolate crumb, tuiles,
  chocolate shapes, Maltesers,
  toasted nuts, mint leaves

For the chocolate parfait
4 egg yolks
100g caster sugar
200g dark chocolate
250ml double cream
200g crème fraîche

For the hazelnut chocolate
  sauce
100g toasted hazelnuts
pinch of salt
150ml double cream
2 tbsp golden syrup
50ml Frangelico
50g dark chocolate, broken into
  small pieces

This made me very, very fat as a child, and it was totally worth it. Okay, this one may not be served in a tall glass in a diner, but it's totally up to you what's in it – just start chucking chocolatey things in your shopping trolley. We like to make a simple chocolate parfait and a nutty sauce. The rest is up to you: feel free to buy it or make it!

For the chocolate parfait, whisk the egg yolks and sugar in an electric mixer or using an electric hand whisk until light and fluffy. Melt the chocolate in the microwave (or in a heatproof bowl set over a saucepan of simmering water, not letting the base of the bowl touch the water). Mix the melted chocolate into the whisked eggs and sugar.

Whip the double cream to soft peaks and fold into the chocolate mixture, then do the same with the crème fraîche. Pour into a plastic tub and freeze for about 2 hours until set.

For the hazelnut chocolate sauce, blend the hazelnuts, with the salt, to a smooth paste in a food processor. Put the cream, golden syrup and Frangelico in a saucepan and bring to the boil. Remove from the heat, then stir in the chocolate and the hazelnut paste until the chocolate has melted and the sauce is smooth.

Lay out all the ingredients and let your guests build their own masterpiece – just make sure you're ready for the mess in the morning!

CAMBRIDGESHIRE BURNT CREAM WITH HOPS AND MALTED-MILK BISCUITS

SERVES 6

200ml whole milk
400ml double cream
1 tbsp malt extract
1 tsp dried hops
5 egg yolks
30g caster sugar
granulated sugar, for sprinkling
crystallised ginger, to serve (see page 60 if you want to try making your own)

For the malted-milk biscuits
125g soft unsalted butter
90g caster sugar, plus extra for dusting
1 egg
2 tbsp Ovaltine
325g self-raising flour
1 tsp salt

Our days on tour usually include an adventure: a trip to the local attractions of the area, a picnic somewhere interesting, paintballing or perhaps a trip into central London. We do, however, love a good trip to a brewery – and after some extensive and potentially excessive research, a.k.a. beer tasting, we have come up with a rather nice dessert using hops. Nostalgic malted milk biscuits (a childhood favourite) go incredibly well with this one. We like to call this a Cambridgeshire Burnt Cream as it's closer to our hearts than its very similar cousin, the crème brûlée.

For the malted-milk biscuits, cream the butter and sugar in an electric mixer until light and creamy, then add the egg, beating until incorporated. Add the Ovaltine, flour and salt and keep mixing until a dough forms. Shape the dough into a log about 10cm thick, wrap in clingfilm and chill in the fridge for 1 hour.

Meanwhile, for the burnt creams, preheat the oven to 110°C. In a saucepan, bring the milk, cream and malt extract to the boil, then remove from the heat and chuck in the hops. Leave to cool and infuse for 10 minutes. In a bowl, mix the egg yolks and caster sugar together. Strain the hop-infused cream into the bowl through a sieve. Mix thoroughly, then pour into 6 ramekins. Place the ramekins in a deep baking dish or roasting tray and pour in enough hot water from the kettle to come halfway up the sides of the ramekins. Cover the whole lot with foil, then bake in the oven for about 30 minutes, or until set but with a slight wobble in the middle. Remove the ramekins from their water bath and chill in the fridge for at least 2 hours.

Immediately increase the oven temperature to 150°C and line a baking tray with baking parchment. Slice the log of biscuit dough into discs and place them on the baking tray. Bake for 15 minutes, or until very light golden. Remove from the oven and cool on a wire rack, then sprinkle with a bit of caster sugar.

When ready to serve, sprinkle the creams with granulated sugar and blowtorch or grill until the sugar is caramelised and almost burnt in places. Serve with the malted-milk biscuits and some crystallised ginger.

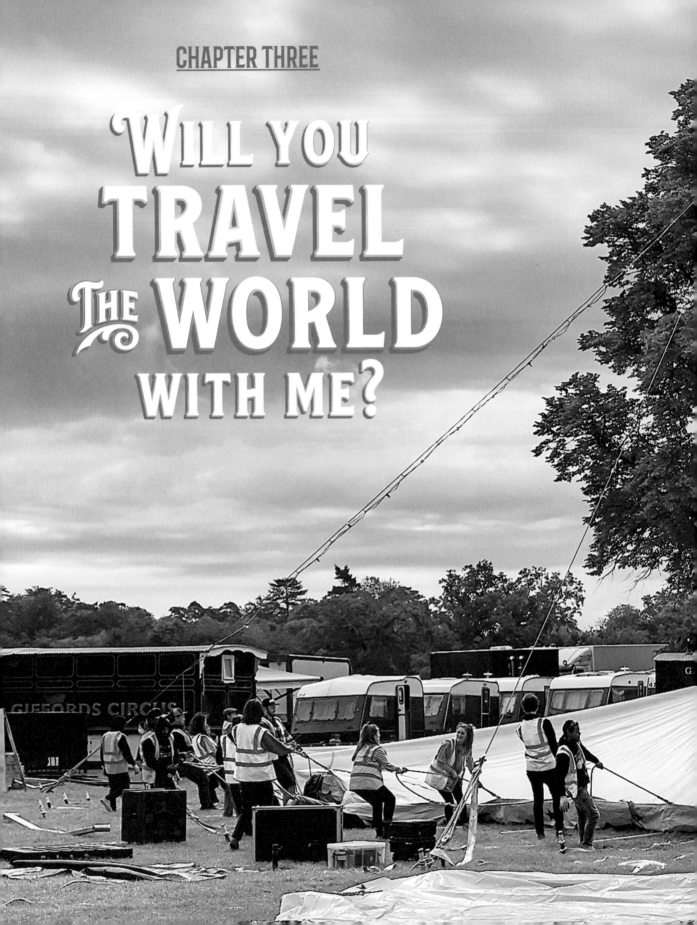

CHAPTER THREE

WILL YOU TRAVEL THE WORLD WITH ME?

The peak of spring intoxication: horse chestnuts presenting waxy candles to an endless sky, cow parsley frothing on the roadside, the sweet lime green of leaves unfurling in a sun that is properly warm. They used to say 'Never cast a cloud until May is out,' but as we leave the farm in mid-May, it feels as if we are leaving the last of winter behind – the last cold breaths, the last cold toes, the last evening chills. As we roll the wagons along warm tarmac to a series of bucolic and beautiful grounds, this is like the honeymoon of the season.

Fast-forged friendships are sealed as we take to the road. Costumes are swapped for high-visibility jackets, work gloves and steel-toe-capped boots. Tempers and manners are tested as we pack our caravans and take our secure little village apart. The Giffords Circus restaurant tent is the first to be taken down and moved. Ols has his own HGV license and he drives the two big restaurant lorries. By mid-morning his team of sous chefs, pastry chefs and crew are already packed and on the road; they are the first to arrive at each ground (or 'stand', in circus terms). The team then set about putting up the restaurant tent, placing the big wooden tables, hanging the decorations and, most importantly, cooking supper for the rest of the company, due to arrive late in the afternoon. Ols prepares a pound-stretching cauldron of Irish stew cobbler. From about six o'clock, the rest of the circus starts to roll in, their faces streaked with make-up and dust and sweat. A queue forms for the seemingly bottomless stew, and soon the restaurant is full of circus people speaking 14 languages – laughing, swearing and comparing notes on their first move. It is a uniquely merry supper, a true dinner party, circus-style.

A QUEUE FORMS FOR THE SEEMINGLY BOTTOMLESS STEW, AND SOON THE RESTAURANT IS FULL OF CIRCUS PEOPLE SPEAKING 14 LANGUAGES -- LAUGHING, SWEARING AND COMPARING NOTES ON THEIR FIRST MOVE.

WE THANK OUR LUCKY STARS THAT GOD, LIFE AND THE UNIVERSE HAVE SOMEHOW DROPPED US IN THESE VERDANTLY BEAUTIFUL PARKS AND GARDENS, PUT MONEY IN OUR POCKETS AND GIVEN US A PARADISE TO PLAY IN.

The next day, the company awakes to build-up day. The tent master rallies the team as they bang in stakes, drag canvas from the lorries and hoist the main (king) poles of the tent. At 11 o'clock everyone stops for their first move-day breakfast – and what a breakfast! Kedgeree is served up to the hungry horde. There are röstis with hot-smoked trout from Bibury Trout Farm, as well as wilted spinach and roast field mushrooms for the vegans, and jugs of elderflower cordial and coffee to drink.

Once the circus is built, the company have a 24-hour break. We thank our lucky stars that God, life and the universe have somehow dropped us in these verdantly beautiful parks and gardens, put money in our pockets and given us a paradise to play in. We join the locals in the nearby pubs, scour the charity shops, catch up on old friendships. The hearty run, the less hearty lounge; books are read, love stories are written and our sleep is full of dreams. The chefs, led by the tireless Ols, investigate the food suppliers of the area, ready for the week ahead – trout from Bibury for a sort of West Country gravadlax, beef from Lambournes in Stow-on-the-Wold to make steak tartare or hot treacle-cured ribeye. Heavy heads of elderflower are cut for elderflower trifle, to be served with berries and mint.

WE JOIN THE LOCALS IN NEARBY PUBS, SCOUR THE CHARITY SHOPS, CATCH UP ON OLD FRIENDSHIPS.

IRISH STEW COBBLER

ON THE CAMPFIRE

SERVES 4

100g butter
4 cuts of lamb neck, on the bone
2 lamb chumps, each sliced in half
50g plain flour
2 onions
1 leek, well washed and sliced
2 carrots, cut into chunks
2 celery sticks, sliced
2 potatoes, peeled and roughly sliced
330-ml bottle of cider
herbs, such as thyme, rosemary, bay leaves, lavender, or whatever's on the allotment
500ml chicken stock
½ quantity Soda Bread dough (page 220)
sea salt and black pepper
chopped parsley, to serve

This is the one-pot wonder we put on as soon as we arrive on-site, then let it tick over while we get organised. Our hunter-gatherer instincts come to the fore as we build a fire and bring out the cauldron, long-famed in Giffords Circus folklore.

Get the cauldron (or a cast-iron pot) nice and hot over the fire or over medium-high heat on the stove, then add half the butter and let it melt. Dredge the lamb in the flour, then brown it in batches in the melted butter and set aside.

In the same pot over low heat, sauté the vegetables in the rest of the butter with a good pinch of salt and pepper until slightly softened. Pour in the cider to loosen any bits stuck to the bottom of the pot. Re-introduce the browned lamb and the herbs. Add the stock, cover with a lid and let it simmer gently for 2 hours, keeping an eye on the fire.

When the lamb is about to fall apart, roll individual pieces, the size of golf balls, of the Soda Bread dough and nestle them into the bubbling stew, then cover and cook for a further 30 minutes with the lid on.

Garnish with chopped parsley, then serve in enamel bowls – and don't forget to crack open a Guinness.

SMOKED HADDOCK KEDGEREE
WITH DUCK EGGS AND SAMPHIRE

SERVES 6

400-ml tin of light coconut milk
1 tbsp garam masala
1 tsp ground turmeric
1 side (500g) natural smoked
   haddock fillet, skinned
200g samphire
300g basmati rice, rinsed
peanut oil, for deep frying
2 shallots, thinly sliced into rings
handful of parsley leaves
6 soft-boiled duck eggs,
   shelled and halved
3–4 radishes, thinly sliced
lemon wedges, to serve

Kedgeree was brought back from colonial India by Scottish troops, travelling from East to West with an abundance of new ingredients and exotic spices. Herbs, rice and spices combine so well with the native flavours of smoked haddock and parsley, and lemons from Europe. We've taken this version slightly further east than Scotland!

In a saucepan, mix the coconut milk with the spices and 200ml water and bring to a rolling simmer. Add the haddock and cook for about 6–7 minutes or until it just starts to flake, then remove from the pan and set aside until needed. Add the samphire and blanch for 3 minutes before removing and setting aside with the haddock.

Add the rice to the pan, cover with a lid and simmer for 10 minutes until cooked through. Remove from the heat but leave the lid on for 5 minutes, so the rice steams and goes fluffy.

Add a good amount of peanut oil in a heavy-based frying pan over high heat, then fry the shallots, stirring vigorously until golden. Throw in the parsley leaves just before the shallots are ready to come out and then drain on some kitchen paper.

Stir the haddock and samphire into the rice and gently warm through over low heat. Spoon onto plates and top with the duck eggs, radishes, crispy shallots and parsley. Serve with lemon wedges.

OVER-RIPE BERRY AND CHAMPAGNE SOUP WITH TOASTED OATS

SERVES 4

500g over-ripe berries
125ml Champagne
4–5 mint leaves
a little golden syrup (optional)
2 handfuls of jumbo oats
knob of butter
crème fraîche and fresh berries,
    to serve

YOU KNOW WHEN YOU'VE PICKED TOO MANY BERRIES AND THEY START TO TURN, THEY'RE SICKLY SOFT, OVERLY SWEET AND WEEPING WITH JUICE? IS THERE A BOTTLE OF FLAT CHAMPAGNE LEFT ON THE TABLE FROM THE NIGHT BEFORE? WHAT DO YOU DO WITH THEM? DON'T JUST TURN THEM INTO JAM! THIS SOUP IS THE PERFECT START TO A SLOW, HAZY SPRING MORNING AFTER A CELEBRATION.

Pop the berries, champagne and mint into a blender and whizz until smooth. Give it a taste and, if it could do with being a bit sweeter, add a little golden syrup.

Toss the oats in a skillet or heavy-based frying pan over low heat with a knob of butter and cook for 5–10 minutes until nice and golden.

Serve the soup in bowls with the oats, a dollop of crème fraîche and some fresh berries.

BEETROOT RÖSTI
WITH HOT-SMOKED TROUT

SERVES 2–4

2 Maris Piper potatoes
1 beetroot
glug of white wine vinegar
knob of butter
2 x 100-g fillets hot-smoked
    trout
2 handfuls of baby spinach,
    washed
4 large, very fresh eggs
rapeseed oil, for frying
sea salt and black pepper
Hollandaise Sauce (page 224)
    and chervil sprigs, to serve

A lavish breakfast, it has to be said… We'll make this when there's a circus birthday – before reminding everyone there's work to do!

Preheat the oven to 160°C and line a baking tray with baking parchment.

Peel the potatoes and beetroot, then grate them into a bowl with a decent amount of salt and pepper. Mix well then make 4 equal-sized nests, about 3cm deep, on the baking tray. Bake the röstis in the oven for 10 minutes until cooked through, then remove and leave to cool. (You can keep these in the fridge until needed, for up to 3 days.)

Put a saucepan of water on to boil and add the white wine vinegar and a pinch of salt.

In a large skillet or frying pan over medium heat, fry the röstis in a drizzle of oil until golden brown and crisp. Add the smoked trout to one side of the pan, with a knob of butter, and let it warm through for a minute or two, then lift out the röstis and trout and drain on kitchen paper. Add the spinach to the same frying pan, together with a turn of salt and pepper, and cook until wilted.

Meanwhile, turn the boiling water down to a simmer and crack the eggs into it, holding them as close to the water as possible. Poach for 2 minutes, then drain on kitchen paper.

To serve, place 1–2 crisp röstis, a mound of wilted spinach, some flaked trout and 1–2 perfect poached eggs on each plate. Finish with a spoonful of Hollandaise Sauce and some mellow chervil sprigs.

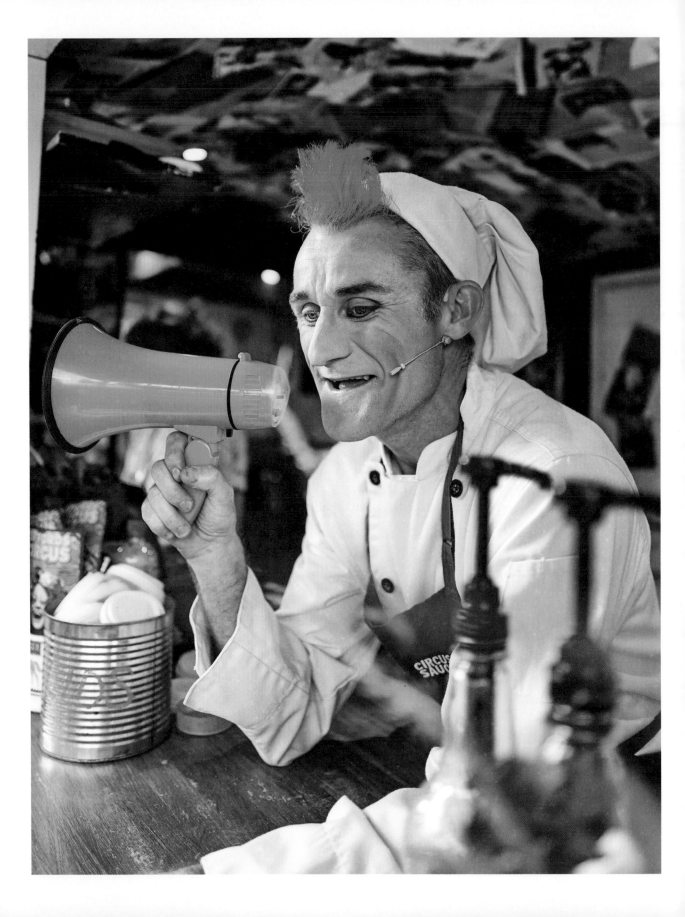

A CLASSIC -- BUT ONLY
FOR THE BRAVEST DINERS!

STEAK TARTARE

SERVES 6

500g rump steak, preferably from the local butcher
6 lengths of marrowbone, sawn in half lengthways – ask your butcher to do this
about 12 thin slices of stale sourdough
6 egg yolks, from very fresh eggs, sitting in their shells
1 small bunch of parsley, leaves picked and finely chopped
1 shallot, very finely chopped
50g cornichons, very finely chopped
50g Lilliput capers
sea salt and black pepper
lemon halves, to serve

For the tartare base
2 egg yolks, from very fresh eggs
1 tsp Dijon mustard
1 tsp balsamic vinegar
150ml vegetable oil
150ml olive oil, plus extra for drizzling
5 green peppercorns in brine
1 anchovy, finely chopped
1 tsp tomato ketchup
1 garlic clove, crushed
juice of ½ lemon
dash of Worcestershire sauce
dash of Green Tabasco (see page 61 for homemade)

The quality of the beef really shines through here, so you can't use any old cut or quality of meat – you just won't get away with it. We like serving this with bone marrow (simply roasted with sea salt), some pickles and all the bits for everyone to get involved with.

Pop the beef in the freezer for an hour to firm up, so it will be easier to slice and dice later.

First off is the tartare base: this gives flavour, heat and tang to the meat and is much like a mayonnaise. Put the egg yolks, the mustard and vinegar in a food processor and mix together. With the processor running, slowly drizzle in both oils to make a stiff mayonnaise. Chop the peppercorns by hand, using the back of the knife to crush them first, then add to the mayonnaise, along with the anchovy, ketchup, garlic, lemon juice, Worcestershire sauce and Green Tabasco to taste.

Preheat the oven to 180°C.

Scrape any excess fat and gristle off the marrowbone using a small knife. In a frying pan over medium heat, colour the marrow side of the bone until golden, then turn back over and season well with salt and black pepper. Transfer to the oven and roast on a baking tray for 20 minutes until caramelised and golden. Turn the oven down to 160°C.

Spread out the slices of sourdough on 2 large baking trays. Drizzle with olive oil and season with salt and pepper, then bake for 15 minutes, until crisp and golden.

Next it's time for the beef: you want to dice it relatively small, without turning it into mince. Put the diced beef in a bowl, drizzle with olive oil and season lightly with salt and pepper. Spoon it onto 6 individual boards or plates, shaping it into a rough ball, and carefully perch an egg yolk in its shell on top. Place small mounds of the parsley, shallot, cornichons and capers alongside the beef. Serve with the roasted bone marrow, a small bowl of the tartare base, a lemon half and sea salt.

Now get stuck in! Mix it all up with a squeeze of lemon juice and scrape onto the crisp sourdough with the bone marrow to whet your appetite for the main course.

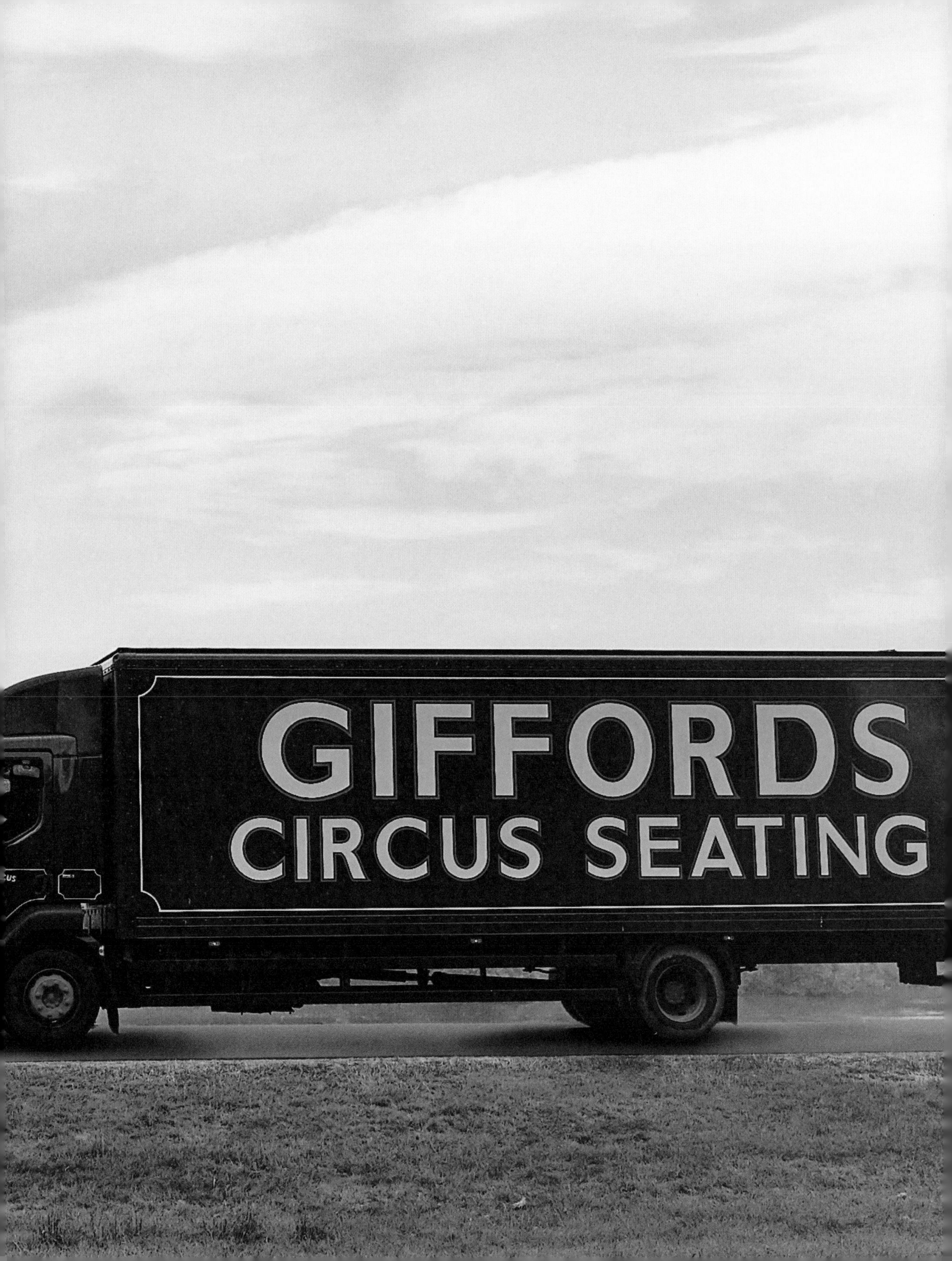
GIFFORDS
CIRCUS SEATING

TROUT CURED IN CABBAGE, GIN AND JUNIPER

WITH CRÈME FRAÎCHE AND RYE CRACKERS

A lovely alternative to smoked salmon using ingredients that you can find in close proximity to your home if you happen to have an allotment and live near a river. The flavour is sweet and salty with a strong aromatic tinge from the gin and juniper.

SERVES 8–10

200g fine sea salt
100g dark brown sugar
4 juniper berries
1 tsp black peppercorns
50ml gin
1 small red cabbage, roughly
   chopped
2 x 1-kg sides of brown, river
   trout, scaled, filleted and
   pin-boned
crème fraîche and lemon halves,
   to serve

For the rye crackers

250g rye flour
250g wholemeal flour, plus extra
   for dusting
1 tsp salt
275ml whole milk
2 egg yolks
100g mixed seeds

In a food processor, blend the salt, sugar, juniper berries, peppercorns, gin and red cabbage to a paste.

Lay one of the sides of trout skin-side down in a deep tray or sealable food container. Smother the flesh side with the paste, then pop the other side on top, skin side up, cover and place in the fridge. Move the fish around every 12 hours, checking its firmness. Depending on the thickness of the fish, it should be ready in about 2 days: you want it to be firm to the touch, without any wobble – if you are unsure, leave it a bit longer.

When the fish is ready, rinse off the paste under cold running water and pat dry with kitchen paper, ready for slicing. The trout will keep in the fridge for at least a couple of weeks.

For the rye crackers, whack both flours and the salt into an electric mixer fitted with the dough hook and mix on a medium speed. In a jug or bowl, whisk the milk and 1 of the egg yolks together, then slowly add to the mixer and keep mixing until you have a firm dough. Wrap in clingfilm and leave to rest in the fridge for 30 minutes.

Preheat the oven to 160°C and line 2 large baking trays with baking parchment.

Roll out the dough into long, thin strips, ideally using a pasta machine, or a rolling pin on a lightly floured surface. Cut the crackers into your desired shape – the larger the better, we find. Lay them out on the baking trays and brush with the remaining egg yolk before sprinkling the seeds over and baking for 10–15 minutes, until crisp and golden.

To serve, slice the trout with a long, thin carving knife, then serve with crème fraîche, lemon halves and, of course, the rye crackers.

Nordic in a West Country kind of way.

TREACLE-CURED RIBEYE
WITH GREMOLATA

SERVES 4–6

1kg joint of beef ribeye
vegetable oil, for frying
rock salt

For the brine
1 litre apple juice
100g black treacle
1 tbsp Marmite
150g salt
100g soft brown sugar
75g ginger, unpeeled and
    roughly sliced
4 garlic cloves, crushed with
    the back of a knife
2 star anise

For the gremolata
1 lemon
3 garlic cloves, peeled
bunch of parsley, leaves picked

The colour and charring around the beef that this cure produces is wonderful – both sweet and slightly fatty from the eye in the middle of the beef. The gremolata cuts through the richness brilliantly: usually, it consists of equal parts lemon zest, garlic and parsley, however I like a little more parsley in mine. We cook the beef very slowly at a low temperature to keep it tender and stop it from tensing.

Put all the ingredients for the brine in a stainless-steel saucepan and bring to the boil, then pour into a deep bowl or plastic tub and leave to cool. Lower the ribeye into the cooled brine and leave to cure in the fridge for at least 24 hours and up to 5 days.

When you're ready to cook the beef, preheat the oven to 150°C. Remove the cured ribeye from the brine and pat dry with kitchen paper. Season with salt and sear on all sides in a hot, ovenproof frying pan with a drizzle of vegetable oil until it looks almost burnt.

Stick a meat thermometer into the centre of the joint, turn down the oven to just 90°C and cook for 1–2 hours. Keep an eye on it: as soon as the internal temperature of the beef reaches 60°C, remove from the oven and leave to rest for 20 minutes.

Meanwhile, make the gremolata. Using a peeler, take off the lemon zest, avoiding the white pith, then finely dice with a sharp knife. Thinly slice the garlic cloves and roughly chop the parsley before combining all these ingredients. Continue chopping until fine. The smell is enchanting.

Slice the ribeye thinly and serve with the cooking juices from the bottom of the pan, a sprinkle of rock salt and a healthy scattering of gremolata. Smashing!

SPRING CHICKEN
WITH MUSHROOMS AND ASPARAGUS

SERVES 2

1kg spring chicken, with liver
2 rashers smoked bacon
a few knobs of butter
1 red onion, cut into quarters
  and skin left on
250g new potatoes
1 sprig of thyme
150g wild mushrooms
1 garlic clove, finely chopped
200g bunch of asparagus,
  trimmed
300ml chicken stock
sea salt and black pepper

It would be wrong not to exploit the wonderful, if short, English asparagus season. We call Tuesdays and Wednesdays our weekend, as we are always in shows on actual weekends. And this is the dish for a day off under the wagon awning – a substitute circus Sunday!

Preheat the oven to 180°C.

Remove the legs from the chicken, then cut out the thigh bone from the legs, leaving a cavity for stuffing. Chop the liver, season well with salt and pepper and stuff it into the legs, then wrap each one nice and tightly in a rasher of smoked bacon.

Season the crown with salt and pepper, then sear the skin in a hot, ovenproof frying pan with a knob of butter. Remove from the pan. Place the onion in the pan, then rest the crown and legs on top and roast for 30 minutes or until the roasting juices run clear when you pierce the meat with a sharp knife. As the crown is not attached to the legs, the bird will not take as long to cook as a normal roast.

Meanwhile, boil the new potatoes until tender (reserving the pan of water), then peel and fry in a good knob of butter with the sprig of thyme until crisp and well browned. In another frying pan or skillet, fry the mushrooms and garlic in a knob of butter and plenty of salt and pepper until golden brown. Blanch the asparagus in the same water as the potatoes for 2–3 minutes before straining and tossing in butter, salt and pepper.

When the chicken is a wonderful golden colour, remove from the pan and leave to rest for at least 10 minutes before serving.

Pour the stock into the chicken pan and place over medium-high heat, stirring to deglaze. Bring to the boil and let it bubble and reduce to sauce consistency.

Serve right away, with a glass of vino.

TWEEDY'S BANOFFEE PIE
WITH SALTED CARAMEL

SERVES 10

2–3 bananas
50g dark chocolate, grated

For the caramel
400-g tin of sweetened
    condensed milk
100g unsalted butter
1 tsp sea salt
50g caster sugar

For the base
250g digestive biscuits
75g unsalted butter, melted

For the cream topping
100g mascarpone
150ml double cream

For the meringue
2 egg whites
120g caster sugar

To begin with, put the tin of condensed milk into a saucepan of boiling water and simmer for 2–3 hours, keeping an eye on it to make sure it doesn't boil dry. The tin MUST be completely immersed in water at all times. After 2–3 hours, remove from the heat and leave to cool before opening – the milk should have become a thick caramel in the tin.

For the base, blitz the biscuits in a food processor, then mix in the melted butter until they resemble damp breadcrumbs. Spread out evenly in a 20cm springform cake tin, pressing down firmly with the end of a rolling pin to flatten. Chill in the fridge until needed.

Pour the cooled caramel from the tin into a heavy-based saucepan. Add the butter, salt and sugar, then bring to the boil and continue to stir until it has loosened to a sauce consistency. Allow to cool slightly, then spread over the biscuit base as evenly as possible before returning the pie to the fridge to chill for at least an hour.

For the cream topping, whip the mascarpone with the cream until soft peaks form. Spread half of it (saving some for piping on top) over the cooled caramel and neatly lay the banana slices on top. Scrape the rest of the cream topping into a piping bag.

For the meringue, whisk the egg whites to soft peaks, then slowly start sprinkling in the caster sugar, whisking constantly until stiff peaks appear. Scrape the meringue into another piping bag.

Unclip the springform ring from around the pie and remove. Pipe rosettes of meringue in the centre of the pie and in a ring around the edge and blast with a blowtorch until you get that wonderful golden colour and toasted marshmallow smell.

Pipe a ring of the whipped mascarpone cream between the 2 meringue circles, then grate over some dark chocolate to finish.

A diet destroyer, rather addictive, very unhealthy and messy enough to be a perfect weapon for a clown, this is another nostalgic classic with a twist: a touch of salt in the caramel and some light meringue make all the difference. Supposedly invented by the Hungry Monk restaurant in Sussex, the origins of banoffee pie are hotly contested, with American contenders in the frame too.

Elderflower and Berry Trifle

SERVES 6

500ml double cream
fresh berries and sprigs of mint,
  to serve

For the custard
280ml milk
1 vanilla pod, split and seeds
  scraped
4 egg yolks
60g caster sugar
25g plain flour
2 tsp cornflour

For the sponge cake
125g caster sugar
4 eggs
125g plain flour
25g butter, melted

For the tuiles
50g butter, melted
50g icing sugar
50g egg whites (1–2 egg whites)
50g plain flour
50g flaked almonds

For the jelly
6 gelatine leaves
400ml diluted elderflower
  cordial (about 1:4 ratio)
300g mixed berries, such as
  strawberries, raspberries and
  blackberries
a few unsprayed elderflowers
  (optional) and mint leaves

First make the custard. In a saucepan, bring the milk to the boil with the vanilla seeds and pod, then remove from the heat and leave to infuse for 10–15 minutes. Remove the vanilla pod. In a heatproof bowl, whisk the egg yolks and sugar until pale before mixing in both flours, then pour in the hot milk, whisking constantly. Pour the custard back into the saucepan, place over high heat and cook until it thickens, stirring constantly and using a spatula to really get into the corners of the pan.

Once thickened, pour the custard into a bowl or container then press a sheet of clingfilm onto the surface to stop a skin forming and leave to cool in the fridge.

Next up, the sponge cake. Preheat the oven to 160°C and line a baking tray (about 30 × 20cm) with baking parchment. Whisk the caster sugar and eggs in a metal or glass bowl over a pan of simmering water until very light and fluffy, then remove from the heat. Gradually sift in the flour, mixing well to avoid lumps, then stir in the melted butter. Spread onto the baking tray and bake for 10 minutes until light brown. Leave to cool on a wire rack before cutting into 2cm squares.

For the tuiles, increase the oven temperature to 170°C and line a baking tray with baking parchment. Blend the melted butter, icing sugar, egg whites and flour in a food processor until smooth, then pour into a container and chill for 30 minutes. Spread the mixture onto the baking tray in tear shapes a few millimetres thick using a palette knife. Sprinkle with the flaked almonds and bake for 10 minutes until golden. Carefully remove from the tray and leave to cool on a wire rack.

For the jelly, soak the gelatine leaves in cold water for 10 minutes. Warm the cordial in a saucepan over low heat, then whisk in the squeezed-out gelatine leaves until fully dissolved. Pour into 1 large bowl or 6 small ones, then float in a mix of berries, elderflowers, a few mint leaves and a few squares of the sponge cake. Leave in the fridge for at least 2 hours to set.

Whip the double cream to soft peaks. Gently fold half the cream through the custard. Whip the other half of the cream to stiff peaks and spoon into a piping bag. Pour the custard on top of the jelly, then pipe rosettes of cream all over and finish with the tuiles, berries and mint.

The earliest mention of trifle dates back to 1585, in a book called *The Good Huswifes Jewell* – although that was just a flavoured thick cream, a mere shadow of the glorious trifle we know today.

If you're pushed for time, you could use sponge fingers instead, but it really is so much better with cake!

This is a good dessert to make when you get back from picking-your-own at a fruit farm on a slow late-spring day.

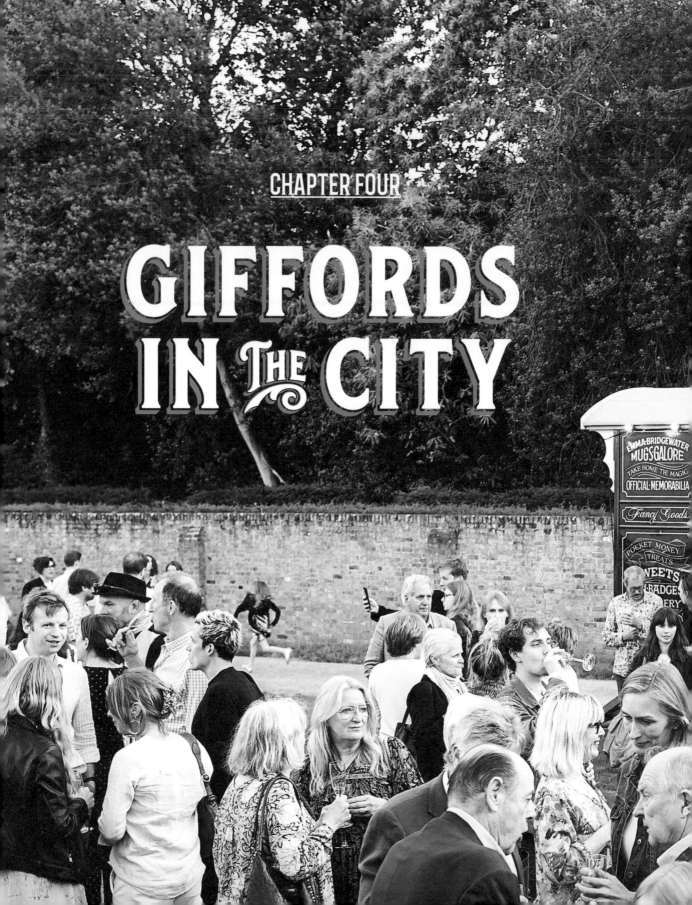

CHAPTER FOUR

GIFFORDS IN THE CITY

By late June, we have found our show, and we feel completely at home in the tent. The musical score and the acts are working together seamlessly and the choreographies have been tapped into muscle memory, like computer code for the nervous system. The circus horses by now know their entrances and exits, and wait in the back with an air of nonchalance. Everyone has learned everyone's names and we're starting to recognise each other by the tone of a voice or the length of a step.

The Cotswold grounds pass swiftly by, and suddenly we are hitching up our caravans and preparing to drive into Oxford and London. For what is essentially a rural touring show, this is city life – and it is thrilling. In Oxford we perform on the lovely park beside Keble College. The city is at our fingertips. There are the smoky, wood-paneled pubs on St Giles, ground well trodden by aesthetes, wanderers and players for generations, centuries even – and, with delight, our musicians follow these spirit paths. The grand Victorian natural history museum is next door, alongside the intriguing Pitt Rivers collection. This is civilisation: nightclubs and swimming pools, string quartets and restaurants. There are rivers to punt on and swim in, a park full of fragrant flowers and a discerning public – I see my old Anglo-Saxon tutor in the crowd.

In the cities, the crowds come thick and fast. Front-of-house steps up to meet the demand for candy floss, and the restaurant adopts a fancier style for the urban crowd. These may be straightforward dishes, but nonetheless are glorious and eye-catching – a sparkling English menu with a circus zest. This is show-off food, pure and simple. The main courses are traditional and theatrical: dressed crab with green Tabasco; salt-baked ham hock with piccalilli; a chicken, leek and truffle pie. As a riff on peach melba, named after an opera singer, we have created a dessert in honour of our very own chanteuse and star, Nancy Trotter Landry. It's a heady creation that marries the chemistry of basil and peaches to such extraordinary effect. We call it Sweet Nancy.

THESE MAY BE STRAIGHTFORWARD DISHES, BUT NONETHELESS ARE GLORIOUS AND EYE-CATCHING -- A SPARKLING ENGLISH MENU WITH A CIRCUS ZEST. THIS IS SHOW-OFF FOOD, PURE AND SIMPLE.

CHISWICK HOUSE OPENING NIGHT

We arrive in Chiswick and set up in the old kitchen garden of Chiswick House. Our menu becomes almost psychedelic in its array of colours: trays of canapés, each more elaborate than the last, are prepared for the opening night. There are rumours circulating of celebrities attending and nerves build with the arrival of the London bustle. It's one hell of an evening.

SALMON GOUJONS
WITH LAVERBREAD TARTARE

SERVES 4–6

500g salmon fillet
1 egg, beaten
300ml whole milk
100g plain flour
200g panko breadcrumbs
50g jumbo oats
vegetable oil, for deep frying
lemon wedges, to serve

For the laverbread tartare
50g cornichons
50g capers
100g laverbread (ask your
   fishmonger for availability)
2 hard-boiled eggs, shelled
300g mayonnaise (see page 139
   for homemade)
juice of ½ lemon
sea salt and black pepper

Goujons are usually made with a white fish like sole or cod, but why? Salmon is a totally different affair! Dip into a tart tartare made with laverbread and you'll never settle for fish fingers again.

For the laverbread tartare, put the cornichons, capers, laverbread and hard-boiled eggs in a food processor and pulse to chop them into coarse chunks, then mix with the mayonnaise and lemon juice. Season to taste.

With a sharp knife, slice the salmon fillet horizontally into 1cm-thick slabs, then slice again into 1cm strips – the length entirely depends on how generous you are feeling!

In a shallow bowl, mix together the egg and milk. Put the flour into another shallow bowl, and the panko breadcrumbs and oats together into a third.

Dust each strip of salmon in the flour, shaking off any excess, then dip into the egg/milk and finally into the bowl of breadcrumbs/oats.

In a deep-fryer or heavy-based saucepan, heat enough vegetable oil to deep-fry the goujons. When the oil has reached 185°C, carefully fry the goujons in batches until golden and crispy, then drain on kitchen paper.

Serve with lemon wedges and the laverbread tartare.

PENNY BUNS

SERVES 8

250ml whole milk
2 tsp caster sugar
225g unsalted butter
50g Cheddar, grated
1 tbsp Marmite
175g plain flour
6 eggs
50g Parmesan, finely grated

For the mushroom filling
100g wild mushrooms or ceps
knob of butter
200g cream cheese
sea salt and black pepper

Penny buns is the English name for cep or porcini mushrooms. We've named these little mushroom-stuffed choux buns after them, because they're similar in shape. They are quite delicious as a canapé or to float in a soup.

Preheat the oven to 190°C and line a baking tray with baking parchment.

Put 200ml water, the milk, sugar, butter, Cheddar and Marmite in a saucepan and bring to the boil. Sift the flour into the saucepan, mixing thoroughly with a wooden spoon and keep beating until a dough forms and starts coming away from the sides of the pan. Transfer the dough to a bowl and leave to cool for a couple of minutes before adding the eggs, one at a time, mixing vigorously with a wooden spoon to incorporate before adding the next. Scrape into a piping bag.

Pipe the pastry onto the baking sheet in 3cm blobs, allowing another 2–3cm between them as they'll expand in the oven. Sprinkle the tops with the grated Parmesan, then bake for 15 minutes, until golden brown. Carefully flip one over and make sure the base is solid enough for you to give it a firm tap. If the buns aren't cooked for long enough, they will just sink again as they cool and it's all rather depressing. Transfer to a wire rack to cool.

For the filling, sauté the wild mushrooms in a searing hot frying pan with a knob of butter until golden, then season with salt and pepper before allowing to cool. Chop coarsely before adding to the cream cheese. Cut each bun in half across the equator and spoon in the mushroom filling.

QUAIL SCOTCH EGGS
WITH BOURBON AND CELERY SALT

MAKES 12

12 quail eggs
knob of butter
2 banana shallots, very finely diced
1 garlic clove, crushed
1 tsp thyme leaves
50ml bourbon whiskey
600g lean minced beef
2 eggs
200ml whole milk
100g plain flour
200g dried breadcrumbs
50g jumbo oats
vegetable oil, for deep frying
sea salt and black pepper
Celery Salt (page 55), for sprinkling

Time to test the homemade Celery Salt with one of the best nibbles known to humankind...

Boil the eggs for 3½ minutes, then shell them.

Melt the butter in a frying pan over medium heat and sauté the shallots with the garlic and thyme until they're soft and opaque. Carefully pour in the bourbon and cook until the alcohol has evaporated. Leave to cool a little, then mix with the beef and season well with salt and pepper.

In a shallow bowl, mix together the eggs and milk. Put the flour into another shallow bowl, and the breadcrumbs and oats together into a third.

Lay out a sheet of clingfilm on a clean work surface, pop a 50g ball of the mince mixture (i.e. one-twelfth of it) on it, then lay another sheet of clingfilm over the top. Roll out with a rolling pin until it looks big enough to coat a quail egg, then do so by removing the top sheet of film and wrapping the mixture around the egg to seal it in completely. Dust the Scotch egg in the flour, shaking off any excess, then dip into the eggs/milk and finally into the breadcrumbs/oats. Repeat with the rest of the mince and eggs.

In a deep-fryer or heavy-based saucepan, heat enough vegetable oil to deep-fry the Scotch eggs. Pour a couple of centimetres of vegetable oil into a small, heavy-based saucepan over medium heat. Heat the oil until a cube of bread dropped into it turns golden in about 15 seconds (about 185°C on a cooking thermometer). Now carefully deep-fry the Scotch eggs in batches until golden and crispy, then drain on kitchen paper.

Leave to rest for a couple of minutes before cutting in half. The yolks should still be runny and the beef medium. Sprinkle with the Celery Salt and order yourself an Old Fashioned!

DRESSED CRAB

WITH ALL THE BITS

SERVES 4

1 large crab, live or cooked
(see method)
8–12 thin slices of stale focaccia
olive oil, for drizzling
3 hard-boiled eggs
50g finely chopped parsley or
dill
1 shallot, very finely chopped
50g Lilliput capers
sea vegetables, to garnish
(ask your fishmonger for
availability)
lemon wedges and Green
Tabasco (see page 61 for
homemade), to serve

For the mayonnaise
1 egg yolk
1 tsp white wine vinegar
1 tsp Dijon mustard
150ml vegetable oil
squeeze of lemon juice
sea salt and black pepper

This is the business. Salivation! Pulling the flesh off a big crab is one of the most satisfying experiences ever (if you love shellfish!), the homemade Green Tabasco is a triumph, and then a squeeze of lemon and a simple mayonnaise is all you need. The rest is really just for show…

Don't try cooking your own crab unless you're confident with crustaceans. If you want to give it a go, get a live crab from the fishmonger and leave it in the freezer for an hour before plunging it into a large pan of salted boiling water. Cook for 15 minutes per kilo, then plunge into ice-cold water.

Now take your crab and extract all the meat from the arms, claws, and body, discarding the feathery grey devil's fingers. Pull out the brown meat from the back of the body and chuck away any fragments of shell, sinew and other odd bits. Return all the meat to the crab shell.

For the mayonnaise, mix the egg yolk with the vinegar and mustard in a bowl. Ever so slowly, trickle in the oil, whisking all the while, until you have a smooth, thick mayonnaise. Season well with salt and pepper and add a good squeeze of lemon juice.

Preheat the oven to 160°C.

Spread out the slices of focaccia on 2 large baking trays. Drizzle with olive oil and season with salt and pepper, then bake for 15 minutes, until crisp and golden.

Separate the boiled eggs into whites and yolks and grate into separate piles around the crab, alongside little piles of parsley or dill, shallot and capers and salt. Garnish with sea vegetables and serve with lemon wedges and Green Tabasco. That's it.

SMOKED HAM HOCK IN PASTRY WITH PICCALILLI

SERVES 4

2 smoked ham hocks
1 onion, roughly chopped
5 cloves
2 star anise
Piccalilli (page 55), dressed
    salad and slices of toasted
    Sweet Potato Bread (page
    221), to serve

For the pastry
500g plain flour, plus extra
    for dusting
pinch of salt
250g chilled unsalted butter,
    cubed
7 egg yolks

Smoked ham hock is a wonderful thing. We sometimes have it with our eggs benedict in the morning if there is spare and it does wondrous things for staff morale. Ham hocks are salted before they are smoked – but not enough for my liking! We like to keep a master stock in the kitchen, and as we use it regularly, the rich, salty brew is infused with flavour from previous braises. You don't need to do this, but it is bloody delicious. For this recipe, we braise the hocks in master stock, then encase them in a buttery pastry to soak up the smoky and salty flavours from the hock.

Put your ham hocks into a stockpot or large saucepan with the onion, cloves and star anise. Pour in enough water (or master stock) to cover, then bring to the boil before turning down to a simmer. Braise for 2½–3 hours until the meat starts to give up but is not yet falling off the bone. Lift the hocks from the pan and leave to drain on a wire rack set over a baking tray.

For the pastry, put the flour, salt, butter, 4 of the egg yolks and 100ml cold water in a food processor and pulse to a breadcrumb consistency. Use your hands to knead into a dough, then wrap in clingfilm and rest in the fridge for at least 30 minutes.

Preheat the oven to 180°C and line a large baking tray with baking parchment. Lightly beat the remaining 3 egg yolks to make an egg wash for the pastry.

Using a sharp knife, peel off the skin of the hocks, leaving a thin layer of fat. On a lightly floured surface, roll out the pastry to a thickness of 8–10mm. Tightly wrap each ham hock in pastry, making an incision to accommodate the bone, then brush the egg wash all over. Place on the baking tray and bake for 20–25 minutes. When it's ready, the pastry should have a bronze sheen to it.

Serve each hock between 2 people with the Piccalilli, a small salad and Sweet Potato Bread toast.

Wilder & More Magical than Ever

CAULIFLOWER, ROMANESCO, RAISIN & ALMOND SALAD

SERVES 4

1 cauliflower
1 head romanesco broccoli
olive oil, for drizzling
2 heads chicory, leaves
    separated
1 shallot, thinly sliced into rings
50g flaked almonds, toasted
sea salt and black pepper

For the purée
knob of butter
100ml double cream

For the dressing
75g raisins
1 tsp Dijon mustard
1 tbsp dark brown sugar
50ml rapeseed oil
1 tbsp cider vinegar

This is a lovely recipe. The raisin dressing adds a wonderful sweetness and cuts through the bitterness of the chicory and the almonds ever so well. Make it!

Preheat the oven to 180°C.

Begin by breaking the cauliflower and romanesco into florets: you want different-sized florets to keep the salad interesting. Save any stalks for the purée. Cook half of the florets in salted boiling water for 4–5 minutes, then drain well. Toss the rest of the florets on a baking tray with a drizzle of olive oil and a sprinkling of salt and roast in the oven for about 10 minutes, until a dark golden colour.

Slice the cauliflower stalks thinly with a sharp knife and sweat down in a saucepan with a knob of butter, and some salt and pepper. Pour in the cream, bring to the boil and blitz in a food processor to a smooth purée. Leave to the side until needed.

For the dressing, soak the raisins in boiling water for about 5 minutes. Drain and put into a mixing bowl with the mustard, sugar, rapeseed oil and cider vinegar. Mix well.

Toss the chicory, shallot, cauliflower and romanesco together in a mixing bowl and season with a little salt and pepper. Smear the purée onto a serving plate and top with the salad. Drizzle over the dressing and finish with a scattering of toasted almonds.

ROAST RACK AND FRIED BREAST OF
LAMB
WITH PEAS AND WILTED LETTUCE

Effectively, this is a spin on lamb, mint and peas... When it's warm enough to sit outside, it's time to visit the local butcher and ransack the allotment. Ask your butcher to chine the lamb rack and French-trim the bones, and to debone the breast. When I think of lamb, this dish is what pops into my head!

SERVES 6

1 breast of lamb, deboned
rapeseed oil, for rubbing and
    frying
1 rack of lamb
a few sprigs of thyme
1 banana shallot, thinly sliced
2 garlic cloves, thinly sliced
100g unsalted butter
handful each of peas, sugar
    snap peas, mangetout,
    chopped lettuce, runner
    beans and broad beans
3–4 mint leaves, torn
squeeze of lemon juice
1 egg
100ml whole milk
100g plain flour
100g panko breadcrumbs
sea salt and black pepper
jus, to serve (optional)

Preheat the oven to 140°C.

Place the lamb breast on a baking tray, rub with a little oil and season with salt and pepper. Roast for 2 hours until very tender. Remove from the oven, place another baking tray on top followed by a weight such as a mortar or heavy pan and leave to chill in the fridge for at least 2 hours.

Meanwhile, increase the oven temperature to 180°C. Put the lamb rack on a chopping board and score the fat to help it render down as it cooks. Season well with salt and pepper. Place the rack, skin-side down, in an ovenproof frying pan over medium heat, along with the thyme, then turn over the lamb when the scored skin has caramelised. You want the lamb to be crisp and golden before turning it over and sealing the other side. When it's nice and brown on both sides, transfer to the oven and roast for 15 minutes, then remove and transfer the pan to a wire rack to rest for 10 minutes.

Sauté the shallot and garlic in a large saucepan over low heat with most of the butter and a good pinch of salt for a couple of minutes, until soft and translucent. Add the peas, lettuce and beans, cover with a lid and cook for 5–6 minutes, stirring every so often. Stir in the remaining butter, the mint and a squeeze of lemon to finish.

In a shallow bowl, mix together the egg and milk. Put the flour into another shallow bowl, and the breadcrumbs into a third. Cut the chilled lamb breast into 6 strips. Dust each strip of lamb in the flour, shaking off any excess, then dip into the egg/milk and finally into the breadcrumbs.

Heat a generous glug of rapeseed oil in a deep frying pan and fry the crumbed lamb pieces until crisp. Drain on some kitchen paper and season well.

Spoon the peas and lettuce onto a platter. Carve the rack of lamb, then arrange on top of the vegetables, along with the crispy strips of lamb breast – and a drizzle of jus, if you have it!

THE SPOILS OF SUMMER!

ROAST CHICKEN, LEEK AND TRUFFLE SUET PIE

SERVES 6–8

2 large leeks, washed, trimmed
  and diced
2 garlic cloves, crushed
2 sprigs of thyme, leaves picked
vegetable oil, for drizzling
1.5kg free-range chicken
50g soft unsalted butter
200ml white wine
500ml double cream
1 bunch of tarragon, leaves
  picked and chopped, plus
  extra whole ones to decorate
1 small fresh truffle, half grated
  and half shaved
small drizzle of good-quality
  truffle oil
sea salt and black pepper

For the suet pastry
400g self-raising flour,
  plus extra for dusting
200g shredded beef suet
10g salt
a few thyme leaves
2 egg yolks, beaten

Preheat the oven to 180°C.

Toss the leeks, garlic and thyme in a drizzle of vegetable oil in a deep roasting tray and season with salt and pepper. Place the chicken on the vegetables, smear with the soft butter, season well, and roast for 1 hour. The bird should be golden and cooked through when done. Leave it to cool slightly, then pick all the meat from the carcass and put to one side.

Set the roasting tray on the hob over medium heat and add the white wine to deglaze it, scraping up any caramelised bits that have stuck to the tray. Boil until the liquid has reduced by half, then add the cream. Once the cream comes to the boil, add the chicken, tarragon, the grated truffle and a tiny drizzle of truffle oil. Season, then remove from the heat and chill in the fridge.

For the suet pastry, put the flour, suet, salt and thyme leaves in a mixing bowl and rub together using your fingers. Transfer to an electric mixer with a dough hook if you have one, or hand-knead it, gradually adding 240ml cold water. Knead for 10 minutes until the suet is incorporated and the dough is smooth and ever so slightly elastic. Wrap in clingfilm and leave to rest in the fridge for 1 hour. Turn up the oven to 190°C.

It's very important that all the ingredients are cold when building the pie; the pastry will act differently if warm. Place the meat filling in a deep ceramic or enamel pie dish. Roll out the pastry on a lightly floured surface until about 1cm thick and large enough to cover the dish with a generous overhang. Brush the underside of the pastry lid with the beaten egg yolk wash and place it over the pie filling to fit snugly, pressing around the sides to ensure it is airtight. Brush more of the egg yolks all over the pastry lid and brush on a few truffle shavings and tarragon leaves to decorate.

Chill the pie in the fridge for 10 minutes, then bake for 25–30 minutes. The pastry should be a shiny golden brown. Finish with a light brushing of truffle oil on top, if you like, and serve with seasonal vegetables and some very creamy mashed potato.

When it comes to pie, we think that, unlike most other meals, the last bite is better than the first, giving the diner a euphoric sense of accomplishment. Kneading the suet pastry helps the pie to rise dramatically, almost like a balloon, and the whiff of fresh truffle when the crust is broken is something quite amazing. Serve this indulgent chicken pie with some simple lightly steamed vegetables.

Queen of Puddings

SERVES 6

500ml whole milk
1 vanilla pod, split and seeds
    scraped
4 egg yolks
60g caster sugar
25g plain flour
2 tsp cornflour
100g panko breadcrumbs
finely grated zest and juice of
    1 lemon

For the fruit jelly
300g mixed berries
    (strawberries, blueberries,
    blackberries and raspberries)
4 leaves gelatine
75g caster sugar
a few strips of lemon zest

For the meringue
130g caster sugar
squeeze of lemon juice
4 egg whites, at room
    temperature
½ tsp cream of tartar

If you've ever had the joy of reading _The Closet of the Eminently Learned Sir Kenelme Digbie Kt. Opened_, published in 1699, you'll find the first printed version of this recipe. There have been many variations since, of course, but it's generally based around bread soaked in milk with jam and meringue – and this is how we do it a few centuries later. After years of serving this in the restaurant, someone only recently pointed out that it looks quite like a crown fit for a queen.

Lightly grease a 20cm springform cake tin and place on a baking tray. In a saucepan, bring the milk to the boil with the vanilla seeds. In a heatproof bowl, whisk the egg yolks and sugar by hand until pale, then mix in the flours. Pour in the hot milk, mixing well all the time, then return to the saucepan. Place over high heat and cook until it starts to thicken, stirring constantly using a spatula to really get into the corners of the saucepan. When the custard has thickened slightly and is almost boiling, take it off the heat and pour into a separate bowl. Stir in the breadcrumbs, lemon zest and juice, then leave to sit for 10 minutes before pouring into the cake tin. Smooth the surface, then set in the fridge for at least 1 hour until cool.

For the fruit jelly, hull and halve the strawberries, then wash all the berries. Soak the gelatine in cold water for 5 minutes. Put the sugar in a medium saucepan with 200ml water and the lemon zest. Bring to the boil, then add all the berries to the syrup and remove from the heat, leave to cool slightly then add the squeezed-out gelatine and stir until completely dissolved. Pour the berry-jelly liquor into the cake tin over the set custard base. Return to the fridge for 1 hour, or until completely set.

For the meringue, put the caster sugar into a saucepan with 100ml water and a squeeze of lemon juice to stop the sugar crystallising. Place over medium heat and bring to 121°C, using a cooking thermometer.

Use an electric mixer to whisk the egg whites with the cream of tartar until soft peaks form. With the mixer running slowly, start adding the hot sugar syrup – the meringue should puff up and stiffen like marshmallow. When all the sugar syrup has been incorporated, keep whisking until the meringue has cooled to room temperature. Scrape into a piping bag fitted with a plain nozzle and pipe over the top of the dessert, then blowtorch or very briefly grill until golden. How can that be from the seventeenth century?!

Sweet Nancy

500g caster sugar
1 cinnamon stick
2 star anise
6 ripe white-fleshed peaches
150g raspberries
Tuiles from page 126, made
  without the almonds
handful of picked basil leaves

For the "ice cream"
200ml condensed milk
300ml cream
1 vanilla pod, split and seeds
  scraped (reserved the scraped
  pod for the peaches)

For the honeycomb
150g caster sugar
100g honey
50g glucose syrup
2 tsp bicarbonate of soda

For the coulis
150g raspberries
finely grated zest and juice
  of 1 lemon

Escoffier was the godfather of French cooking, and so many of his recipes are still used today – among them peach melba, which was first served at the Savoy Hotel to honour the great Australian Soprano Dame Nellie Melba. This version is a homage to the wonderful Nancy Trotter Landry, who has been the ring mistress for many of Giffords performances. If you've ever seen her perform, you'll know why we've named this after her.

First make the "ice cream". Using condensed milk is a bit of a cheat, but why not if you don't have an ice cream machine or any patience to speak of. Beat the condensed milk, cream and vanilla seeds together in an electric mixer fitted with a whisk attachment until stiff peaks form. Pour into a container and freeze for 3–4 hours, by which time it should scoop like real ice cream.

For the honeycomb, line a baking tray with baking parchment. Put the sugar, honey and glucose syrup in a non-stick saucepan over high heat. Let it bubble away until you have a golden caramel and it reaches 113°C on a cooking thermometer. Take off the heat and quickly whisk in the bicarbonate of soda before pouring the volcanic mass out onto the baking tray and hoping for the best. Leave well alone for an hour, then see if the alchemy has succeeded!

For the coulis, in a small bowl mix the raspberries with the lemon zest and juice. Sieve if you don't like the seeds, then chill until needed.

To poach the peaches, bring 500ml water and the sugar to the boil with the cinnamon, star anise and the scraped-out vanilla pod. Add the peaches, lower the heat to a gentle simmer and poach them for 5–10 minutes, depending on their ripeness. When they are tender, take off the heat and leave to sit in the syrup until cool. Peel the cooled peaches, cut them in half and remove the stones, then set aside in the syrup until needed.

Present the peaches on a platter with the "ice cream", coulis, raspberries, Tuiles and some basil leaves – plus shards of the honeycomb, if it lasts that long with Nancy around…

CHAPTER FIVE

HIGH SUMMER
HIGH SPIRITS

We inhale London, and just at the moment when it feels as if we are full, we move on again – out into the lush river valleys and hills between the capital and Oxford. At this point in the summer, we are riding high. Relieved that our big city stand is over, and by now completely sure of what we are doing and who we are, the character of the company is fully formed and we can afford some downtime.

During a two-week stand in Windsor Great Park, we sprawl out under the vast oak trees. Barbeques are held, running clubs are formed. On days off, impromptu sports matches make the most of the summer-evening sun: hilarious three-legged races and absurd feats of strength and stamina. By-now muscled and tanned kitchen staff pit their strength against the circus athletes, the competition and love equally fierce. The circus horses enjoy huge outdoor grazing pens, and we watch the polo ponies scudding across the bright green, irrigated pitches. We marvel at the historic parklands, admiring their secret and ancient trees – like standing giants. Careful management of the deer in the park means that the Windsor farm shop is well stocked with fresh local venison.

We journey on to Henley, and the strawberry season seems endless. Henley's surprisingly good antique and junk shops offer fancy dishes of every sort – the cutlery and canteens of a thousand riverside picnics – and we serve drinks and syllabubs in cut-glass and polished silver plate. Everything has an old-world brilliance and sweetness about it. In celebration of this glut of ingredients and the feeling of every day being a special occasion, Ols rustles up roast guinea fowl and Eton mess.

Visitors to the circus are colourful: our own families, intrepid friends from abroad, billionaires arriving by helicopter. We live in a complete circus bubble, a never-never land with no beginning and no end, and only short shadows needed for company as we are held by the presence of each other and we feel as if we want for nothing.

BY-NOW MUSCLED AND TANNED KITCHEN STAFF PIT THEIR STRENGTH AGAINST THE CIRCUS ATHLETES, THE COMPETITION AND LOVE EQUALLY FIERCE.

BAURU BEEF SANDWICH

SERVES 6–8

1 cottage loaf
Mayonnaise (see page 139 for homemade) and English mustard, for spreading
300g rare roast beef, thinly sliced
2 beefsteak tomatoes, thinly sliced
handful of spinach leaves
2 x 125g balls of mozzarella, sliced

Leftover beef from Sunday lunch and circus the next day? Time to make a Bauru sandwich for a picnic. Just be sure to bring a bread knife!

Preheat the oven to 120°C.

Cut a horizontal slice off the top of the loaf of bread, then dig out the soft inner part and save for making breadcrumbs.

Smear the inside with mayonnaise and mustard, then add layers of the beef, tomatoes, spinach and mozzarella. Wrap in foil and bake for 30 minutes before chucking in your picnic hamper with a wooden board and a bread knife. The loaf should still be warm when you reach the common!

BBQ Corn with Sweet Chilli Butter

SERVES 6

1 red chilli, trimmed and deseeded
2 garlic cloves, peeled
50g dark brown sugar
150g unsalted butter, cubed
6 corn cobs, in their husks
sea salt

Made for the portable BBQ – but don't forget the napkins, as you're guaranteed hot, greasy cheeks after eating these...

Chuck the whole chilli and garlic cloves into a food processor with the sugar and blend to a paste. Add the butter and blend again to incorporate, then spoon into a container.

Get the BBQ on the go, then pull back the husks of the corn and tie with some string so you have something to hold on to whilst eating. Chuck the cobs straight on the barby to cook, keeping a keen eye on them and turning them every so often, until they are evenly charred and feel cooked when pierced with the tip of a knife.

Remove from the BBQ and, using a pastry brush, smother the cobs in the sweet chilli butter, finishing with a sprinkling of sea salt.

DUCK LIVER PARFAIT WITH GUINNESS JELLY AND SODA FARLS

We may have wonderful beer in the West Country, but we're never going to turn down a pint of the black stuff! The tartness of Guinness goes well with this liver parfait, and the quick soda farls create one of our favourite aromas, especially with the butter melting on top (ideally Kerrygold, recommended by our Irish colleagues.) This needs to be eaten with live music, more Guinness, some good craic and even more Guinness…

SERVES 6–8

500g duck livers, at room temperature
250ml whole milk
1 tsp pink salt
50ml port
50ml madeira
2 shallots, thinly sliced
1 garlic clove, thinly sliced
3 sprigs of thyme, leaves picked
1 bay leaf
175g unsalted butter, melted and hot
2 eggs, at room temperature
sea salt and black pepper
watercress, cornichons and Irish butter, to serve

For the Guinness jelly
4 gelatine leaves
200ml Guinness
2 tsp dark brown sugar

For the soda farls
1 quantity Soda Bread dough (page 220)

Begin by soaking the duck livers for 10–20 minutes in the milk with a decent pinch of the salt to remove any bitterness. Meanwhile, put the port, madeira, shallots, garlic, thyme and bay leaf in a saucepan over medium heat and let it bubble away until syrupy and reduced (roughly by a third), then let cool.

Drain the livers in a sieve, then sprinkle with the remaining salt – this helps to stop them discolouring.

Preheat the oven to 110°C.

In batches, blitz the livers, port reduction, butter and eggs in a blender or food processor until smooth, then pass through a sieve and season well. Work quickly, as the parfait can split if it cools too quickly. Pour into ramekins or a terrine mould, then place in a deep baking tray and pour in enough hot water from the kettle to come two-thirds of the way up the sides of the ramekins/mould. Cover the whole tray with foil and bake until the parfait is done but still has a wobble in the middle – about 10–20 minutes for ramekins, 30–40 minutes for a terrine mould. Remove from the tray and refrigerate until needed.

For the Guinness jelly, soak the gelatine in cold water for 10 minutes. Heat the Guinness and brown sugar in a saucepan until the bubbles have gone, then mix in the squeezed-out gelatine, stirring to dissolve it completely. Pour into a small container and put in the fridge for at least 1 hour until set.

If using a terrine mould, tease out the parfait onto a plate with a butter knife and some warm water and return to the fridge for a couple of hours. When cold, cut into thick slices.

Mould the Soda Bread dough into 2 or 3 large balls and flatten them so they're about 2–3cm deep. Heat a dry, heavy-based skillet over medium heat and then add the dough discs and let them do their thing. After 5–6 minutes, flip them over and cook for another 5–6 minutes. Turn out onto a board, slather some butter and a little salt on the top, then cut into wedges.

Turn out the Guinness jelly onto a chopping board and chop finely with a knife.

Serve the parfait and jelly with watercress, cornichons and the steaming-hot soda farls with some more butter. Nothing better!

THE PLOUGHMAN, THE TART AND THE BISHOP

SERVES 6

100g smoked bacon lardons
1 large onion, sliced as thinly as
    possible
1 garlic clove, sliced
2 sprigs of thyme, leaves picked
2 large baked potatoes
250g Stinking Bishop cheese
sea salt and black pepper
pickles, cured meats, salad,
    whatever you can find left
    over in the fridge, to serve...

To my dismay, I discovered that the ploughman's lunch was actually created by a cheese company to increase its sales in the 1950s. I'd always thought it was a cunning, thrifty, intelligent and romantic way of using up leftovers. Which it is, really.

First you need a good pint of ale: Pig's Ear, Hooky Gold or, hey, why not, a Bishop's Finger? Then let's see what's in the fridge or local deli – cured trout, duck liver parfait, terrine, Scotch eggs, salt beef, hay and honey roast ham, pease pudding, greengage chutney, a chunk of Double Gloucester, some celery, apples, pickled onions and whatever else tickles your fancy.

As a centrepiece to all these lovely things, I like to make a version of tart(iflette) from closer to home. Instead of reblochon, we use the famous Stinking Bishop from Dymock in Gloucestershire, a smidge more pongy than the renowned fromage de Haute-Savoie! We can also give it a smutty name…

Fry the bacon lardons in a dry frying pan over medium heat until crisp and golden brown, then use a slotted spoon to lift them out of the pan and set aside. Add the onion, garlic and thyme to the bacon fat in the pan, season with salt and pepper, and cook, stirring frequently, until soft and translucent.

Preheat the oven to 180°C.

Slice the baked potatoes lengthways, trying to keep the slices intact, then do the same with the Stinking Bishop; these are the bricks and mortar of the tart.

Now it's time to build! On a baking tray lined with baking parchment, start layering. A layer of potato first, then Bishop, onion, followed by a sprinkling of lardons. Keep going until everything is used up. Bake for 20–30 minutes, until the cheese has melted and the top is crisp and golden.

Serve the tart(iflette) in the middle of your veritable feast… and pour another ale, for heaven's sake!

GLOBE ARTICHOKES

WITH MUSTARD HOLLANDAISE

SERVES 4

4 whole artichokes
1 tbsp wholegrain mustard
1 tbsp Dijon mustard
1 quantity Hollandaise Sauce
   (page 224)
sea salt and black pepper

Yes, artichokes do make a huge amount of mess, but they're amazing to eat and so simple to cook. A lot of recipes use just the hearts, but for me that's like not eating a boiled egg from the shell – it has a different taste and feel to it.

Peel away a few of the outer leaves from the artichokes. Bring a large saucepan of salted water to the boil, drop in the artichokes and cook for 25–30 minutes until you can push a small knife into the centre.

Meanwhile, stir both mustards through the Hollandaise Sauce and keep warm in a small saucepan over low heat.

Cut the artichokes in half before serving, as the layers of leaves look so beautiful. Serve with a sprinkle of sea salt and black pepper, a bowl of the mustard hollandaise and a basket or bowl for the waste.

To eat, remove each leaf with your fingers, dunk the fleshy end into the hollandaise and suck. Do this until you reach the middle, then scrape out and discard the furry choke and chow down on the heart. There's more work in the eating than the cooking here, but it's so worth it!

LOBSTER & SQUID INK LASAGNE

For when you're feeling generous… A perfect balance of comfort and gluttony make this something to turn heads, for a few quid that is.

SERVES 4

2 x 500g live lobsters
1 tsp fennel seeds
2 garlic cloves, thinly sliced
50ml Pernod
1 tsp English mustard
600ml whole milk
75g unsalted butter
75g plain flour
finely grated zest of 1 lemon
handful of tarragon leaves,
    chopped
150g Parmesan, finely grated
sea salt and black pepper
green salad, to serve

For the squid ink pasta
4 large eggs
2 tsp squid ink
400g '00' flour
1 tbsp salt

First, make the pasta. Mix together the eggs and squid ink until combined. Pile up the flour in a mound on your work surface and mix in the salt, then make a well in the middle. Pour the egg mixture into the well and use your fingers to stir the flour into the eggs, drawing in more and more flour from the mound until you can start kneading. Using the heels of your hands, knead for 10 minutes until the dough is silky-smooth. Wrap in clingfilm and leave to rest in the fridge for at least 30 minutes.

Pop the lobsters in the freezer for 30 minutes to send them to sleep. Plunge into salted boiling water and cook for 15 minutes, then remove from the pan and submerge in cold water to cool. When they are cool enough to handle, extract all the meat, using a rolling pin or the back of a heavy knife to crack the shells. Set both meat and shells aside.

Using a pasta machine, roll out the dough into 2mm-thick sheets and then cut into smaller squares. Bring a saucepan of salted water to the boil, blanch the pasta sheets for 2 minutes then refresh under cold running water and lay out on a clean, dry tea towel.

Preheat the oven to 180°C.

With the rolling pin, bash up the empty lobster shells, then roast in a roasting tray for 20 minutes. Transfer to a saucepan and leave the oven on, ready for the lasagne.

Add the fennel seeds, garlic and Pernod to the saucepan with the shells and cook over medium heat for a couple of minutes before adding the mustard and milk. Simmer for 20 minutes, then pass through a sieve. Melt the butter in a clean saucepan, stir in the flour and cook for 3–4 minutes, stirring constantly. Gradually add the sieved milk, stirring constantly, then simmer over low heat, still stirring, until the sauce thickens. Season to taste with salt and pepper.

Place 4 squares of baking parchment on a baking tray or in individual ovenproof pans. Now start building the lasagnes in stacks on each square of parchment, alternating layers of pasta, lobster meat and sauce, with a scattering of lemon zest, tarragon and Parmesan between layers. Aim for 5–6 layers, finishing with a piece of claw meat and a bit of Parmesan. Bake for 20 minutes, until the cheese is bubbling and golden brown, then serve with a green salad as this is "mighty" rich!

HAM IN HAY

WITH PARSLEY SAUCE

SERVES 8

1.5kg uncooked ham
2 handfuls of washed,
    unsprayed organic hay
6 juniper berries
2 star anise
10 cloves
4 bay leaves
garden shoots and Pickled
    Vegetables (page 53),
    to serve

For the parsley sauce
1 bunch of parsley, leaves picked
1 garlic clove, peeled
50ml double cream
sea salt and white pepper

Another British classic that's perfect for a light starter. Hay has been used for many years to give meat a rather unique flavour. We serve this cold with a parsley sauce and pickled vegetables and it goes down very well in late summer.

Place the ham in a large saucepan with the hay, juniper berries, star anise, cloves and bay leaves, pour in enough water to cover and bring to the boil. Turn down the heat, cover with a lid, and simmer gently for 3 hours, then remove the ham from the liquid and leave to chill in the fridge until cool. Reserve the stock.

For the parsley sauce, blanch the parsley leaves and garlic in a small saucepan of boiling water for 2 minutes, then drain in a sieve. Refresh in cold running water, then drain again, using the back of a spoon to press out as much water as possible. Put the parsley in a blender with the garlic and 100ml of the warm ham stock and blitz to a paste. Add the cream at the end with a good seasoning of salt and pepper.

Slice the ham nice and thinly and serve with some fiery garden shoots and of course some Pickled Vegetables from the larder.

ROAST COD WITH SQUID, SMOKED HOCK AND CHARRED SWEETCORN

SERVES 6

2 smoked ham hocks
1 onion, roughly chopped
5 cloves
2 star anise
6 x 150g cod fillets
olive oil, for frying
150g plain flour
a few knobs of butter
squeeze of lemon juice
2 tsp pink peppercorns,
    lightly crushed
1 tsp smoked paprika
2–3 squid, cleaned, with
    tentacles
fresh kernels from 3 corn cobs
head of red chicory, leaves
    separated
sea salt and black pepper

I think these four things go really well together: meaty cod, smoky and tender ham hock, crisp fried squid and sweet charred corn. This is a 'surf and turf' of distinction, a moreish, comforting dish, which you can serve with either red or white wine. It's also a dish that requires you to visit the fishmonger, butcher and greengrocer... what a way to spend a morning!

Put your ham hocks into a stockpot or large saucepan with the onion, cloves and star anise. Pour in enough water to cover, then bring to the boil before turning down to a simmer. Braise for 3–3½ hours, until the meat starts to fall away from the bone. Remove from the heat and, when the meat is cool enough to handle, pull it off the bones in large flakes.

Preheat the oven to 180°C.

Season the cod well with salt and pepper. In a hot pan with a drizzle of olive oil, place the fish skin-side down and let it cook undisturbed over high heat until the edges of the skin start to go golden. Turn down the heat slightly then whack in a knob of butter and a squeeze of lemon juice, basting the fish with melted butter for 4–5 minutes. Flip over and baste for a further 2–3 minutes. Remove the cod from the pan, leave to rest on a rack and pour the pan juices over the top.

In a shallow bowl, mix together the flour, pink peppercorns, paprika and a little salt and pepper. Slice open the squid hoods and score the inside with a sharp knife, then cut into triangles. Dust all the squid, including the tentacles, in the seasoned flour and shake off the excess. In a heavy-based saucepan, fry the squid over very high heat with a decent amount of oil for 1–2 minutes until crisp and golden. Drain on kitchen paper.

Cook the corn kernels in a dry frying pan over high heat with a little sea salt until it pops and chars. Add a knob of butter to finish.

Serve the cod, squid, corn and ham with the chicory leaves. Accompany with leftover new potatoes, if you have them.

ROAST GUINEA FOWL

WITH HERITAGE TOMATOES, DUMPLINGS AND BLACK-GARLIC AÏOLI

SERVES 6

1 guinea fowl
½ lemon
large handful of garden
  aromatics, such as sage,
  rosemary and thyme
olive oil, for drizzling
6–7 heritage tomatoes, sliced
sea salt and black pepper
toasted pine nuts, dressed
  rocket and Parmesan, to serve

For the dumplings
500g Maris Piper potatoes,
  peeled and cut into chunks
100g plain flour
1 egg, lightly beaten
20g parmesan, grated
a grating of nutmeg
1 tsp salt
butter, for frying

For the black-garlic aïoli
2 egg yolks
4 black-garlic cloves, peeled
juice of ½ lemon
150ml olive oil
150ml vegetable oil

Guinea fowl has a gamier flavour than chicken, and is much nicer when roasted on the bone, as it can be dry otherwise. Having been chased by rampant guinea fowl more than once, I reckon they're also a lot more terrifying than their tamer cousins in the hen house. This makes a lovely late-summer dish to go with the ripest of tomatoes and some basil gnocchi.

Preheat the oven to 180°C.

For the dumplings, put the potatoes on to cook in a saucepan of salted boiling water for about 15 minutes until you can easily slip the tip of a knife right through to the centre. Drain, put back in the pan over low heat and leave to steam for a few minutes before mashing with a potato masher. Once the potato has cooled slightly, add the flour, egg, Parmesan, nutmeg and salt and mix together. Leave until needed.

Stuff the cavity of the guinea fowl with the lemon half and sit it in a baking tray on a bed of garden aromatics. Drizzle generously with olive oil and season with salt and pepper, then roast for 25–30 minutes, until the juices run clear when the tip of a knife is inserted into the thickest part of the thigh. Leave to rest for 10 minutes.

Meanwhile, for the black-garlic aïoli, put the egg yolks, garlic, lemon juice and a good pinch of salt in a food processor and whizz briefly to combine. With the machine running, slowly trickle in the oils. When all the oil has been incorporated, you should have a rich, glossy aïoli. Season to taste.

Fry the dumplings in a heavy-based skillet over low-medium heat with a good amount of butter until firm and showing a good amount of colour on all sides. Leave to drain on kitchen paper until needed.

Arrange the tomatoes on a platter, seasoning them well with salt and pepper. Carve the guinea fowl and lay it on top of the tomatoes, then scatter the fried dumplings around the bird. Finish with toasted pine nuts, some dressed rocket and grated parmesan, and a drizzle of the black-garlic aïoli.

BLACK FOREST TRIFLE

SERVES 8

250g Chocolate Brownies (page 51) cut into small cubes
250ml double cream
125g mascarpone
50g icing sugar
1 quantity Tuiles (page 126), optional
cocoa powder, to serve

For the chocolate crème pâtissière
280ml whole milk
4 egg yolks
60g caster sugar
25g plain flour
2 tsp cornflour
25g dark chocolate, chopped, plus extra for grating

For the cherry jelly
75g caster sugar
50ml kirsch
300g cherries, pitted and halved (but keep a handful whole, to finish)
6 gelatine leaves

When cherries come into season it's all too easy to demolish them by the punnet, leaving you with stained lips and fingers. But there are so many other ways to enjoy cherries: Schwarzwälder Kirschtorte is the romantic-sounding German 'Black Forest' cake dating from the nineteenth century that has been the basis for many different chocolate and cherry confections over the years. Here we've gone for a trifle, and it works rather well.

First make the chocolate crème pâtissière so that it has time to cool. In a saucepan, bring the milk to the boil. In a heatproof bowl, whisk the egg yolks, sugar and both flours with a balloon whisk until pale, then pour in the hot milk, whisking constantly. Pour the custard back into the pan over high heat and cook until it thickens, stirring constantly and using a spatula to really get into the corners of the pan. Stir in the chocolate and when it has melted, remove from the heat and pour into a clean bowl. Press a piece of clingfilm onto the surface to prevent a skin forming, then refrigerate.

For the cherry jelly, bring the sugar, 400ml water and the kirsch to the boil and drop in the pitted and halved cherries, then take off the heat and leave to sit. Soak the gelatine in cold water for 10 minutes, then squeeze out and add to the cherry liquor while still hot, stirring to dissolve. Pour the jelly mixture into a serving bowl and drop in the Chocolate Brownie cubes. Leave to set in the fridge for 1 hour.

Whisk the cream, mascarpone and icing sugar to soft peaks. Put half into a piping bag fitted with a plain nozzle.

Take the cooled crème pâtissière out of the fridge and stir with a spatula to loosen. Gradually incorporate the other half of the whipped cream, folding it in gently with your spatula until smooth. Spoon into the serving bowl on top of the jelly and smooth over with a hot spatula, saving some to pipe.

Pipe on both types of cream in little peaks, then finish with the reserved whole cherries, some grated chocolate and possibly even some Tuiles dusted with cocoa powder, if you fancy.

ETON MESS

SERVES 6

300g strawberries
75g caster sugar
strips of lemon zest
1 vanilla pod, split and seeds
    scraped
400ml double cream
200g mascarpone

For the meringue
6 egg whites
230g caster sugar
230g icing sugar

PICTURE THE SCENE: Eton v Harrow, in 1893, on the cricket pitch – this is when this dessert is commonly thought to have first been served. Since then, it has become a firm favourite across the nation. The most important element of an Eton mess is the strawberries, which must be the finest you can get. A close second is the meringue. Yes, you could easily use shop-bought meringues, but they won't be nearly as good as these chewy, crunchy ones you can make yourself. And the mascarpone gives the cream a wonderful richness and smooth finish.

For the meringue, preheat the oven to 120°C and line a large baking tray with baking parchment.

In an electric mixer, whisk the egg whites until the whites begin to froth and are almost at the soft-peak stage, then begin slowly tapping in the caster sugar, while still whisking. Keep whisking until the meringue is super thick, then remove the bowl from the mixer. Gradually sift in the icing sugar, folding it in gently and ensuring there are no lumps of sugar left. Spoon or pipe the meringue onto the baking tray in one single shape and bake for 2 hours, or until slightly coloured and very crisp.

The rest is very simple. Put half the strawberries in a heatproof bowl with the sugar, lemon zest and scraped vanilla pod, cover tightly with clingfilm and poach over a pan of simmering water for about 30 minutes until the strawberries start to shrivel. Doing it this way keeps all the flavour in and when you pop that clingfilm open, you get the most miraculous smell! Remove the vanilla pod and strips of zest and blend a few large spoonfuls of the strawberries in a blender to make a coulis, then put this and the rest of the strawberries in the fridge to chill until needed.

In a large bowl, whip the cream, mascarpone and vanilla seeds to stiff peaks. Add most of the fresh strawberries, hulled and halved, and crumble in nearly all the meringue. Pile onto a dish or cake stand and scatter over the poached strawberries, followed by more fresh strawberries, more meringue and finally the coulis. Pour another glass of Pimm's and enjoy the game! Toodle pip!

To my mind, Eton mess just has to be eaten outside in the sun, with a pitcher of Pimm's. If there's any left after service, we send a message out to all the performers and it's not long before several faces begin to appear at the back door, ready to dive in!

CUSTARD TART

•——•

WITH NUTMEG AND POACHED RHUBARB

SERVES 8–10

½ quantity Shortcrust Pastry, made following the instructions on page 45 and blind-baked in a greased 20cm fluted tart tin
4 whole eggs
2 egg yolks, plus an extra one for glazing
150g caster sugar
400ml double cream
200ml whole milk
a grating of nutmeg
Poached Rhubarb (page 33), to serve

A custard and nutmeg tart should not be messed with – it's one of those wondrous things that cannot be bettered, apart perhaps from a little poached rhubarb on top. The main pitfalls are soggy pastry or over- or under-cooking the custard, so you need to be on the ball.

Leave the oven on at 170°C after blind baking the pastry.

As the custard filling for this recipe is fairly liquid when it goes into the oven, you need a well-sealed tart shell, with no holes, cracks or weaknesses. To be on the safe side, brush the blind-baked tart shell with the extra yolk for glazing, and pop the tart shell back in the oven for 5 minutes – this will ensure that no liquid can seep through. Remove the tart shell from the oven and reduce the temperature to 120°C.

Whisk the eggs, yolks and sugar together in a heatproof bowl with a balloon whisk. Pour the cream and milk into a saucepan and bring to the boil, then pour slowly into the whisked egg bowl and whisk vigorously until combined. Pass the custard through a sieve into a jug, then pour into the tart case until just shy of the rim of the shell. Give the tart a gentle shake to dispel any air bubbles, then liberally dust with grated nutmeg.

Very carefully slide the tart into the oven and bake for 45 minutes–1 hour, until the custard is set but still has a satisfying wobble. Leave to cool in the fridge – this helps to prevent the surface from cracking.

That's it... yes, it's been done many times before, but a good custard tart is just incredible. Serve with some Poached Rhubarb.

CHAPTER SIX

CIRCUS NIGHTS AND CIRCUS DAYS

The school holidays start and we turn towards home, reluctantly leaving behind the banks of the Thames and heading back to the Cotswold hills. The number of shows per week intensifies to meet the demand for the circus in July and August. There is a feeling that the honeymoon of the season is over and the real graft starts.

Tensions are felt in the company and have to be negotiated. Ready for this mid-season dip, the company old-timers and stalwarts organise film screenings in the tent and swimming trips to nearby lakes. But mainly this is a time of shows and more shows, for it is high season and there is a non-stop flow of holiday-makers, tourists and farming families. It is their curiosity and enthusiasm that keep us going. An ecstatic audience lifts us.

We are more frugal with our free time, and this is a period of shared suppers – caravan food to sustain us. By now, everyone is completely accustomed to their caravan or bunk living spaces and have customised them in turn: a crate nailed to the outside of a caravan as a handy drying rack; an awning carefully positioned to shelter a television, satellite dish and pot plants. One night our head horse trainer, Dany Cesar, hosts a little supper for some friends in the stable tent, humans and animals relaxing and eating in quiet conviviality, the tent walls lifted, the air warm and still. (Dany is Belgian but lives in Spain. Being a circus person and having lived an itinerant life, he knows people everywhere – this particular evening the assembled company includes a wild-animal trainer from Chipping Norton.)

The velvet nights after the shows, when the crowds have gone home and the air is warm but not boiling, are our golden moments. For the company, some of them perhaps more used to a tropical way of life, these are the treasured little parcels of time when make-up, costumes, fishnets, cooks' whites and work clothes are finally shed and everyone relaxes. There is no energy now for restaurants and pub crawls, so we all cook – for ourselves and each other – and caravan suppers, being essentially thrifty, small-space feasts, are perfected. In the restaurant, the food is languid and delicious.

IT IS HIGH SEASON AND THERE IS A NON-STOP FLOW OF HOLIDAY-MAKERS, TOURISTS AND FARMING FAMILIES. IT IS THEIR CURIOSITY AND ENTHUSIASM THAT KEEP US GOING. AN ECSTATIC AUDIENCE LIFTS US.

DIRTY, SMOKY, FILTHY FRIES

SERVES 4

vegetable oil, for deep frying
1 large potato
1 large sweet potato
50g potato flour (optional)
4 rashers smoked bacon
sea salt and black pepper
100g paprika mayonnaise
    (page 33)
thinly sliced spring onions,
    grated cheddar and pickled
    jalapeños, to serve

Americana… it's got to happen. You can't eat like this every day, so make the most of these filthy fries!

Heat the vegetable oil in a deep-fat fryer or heavy-based saucepan to 140°C. Cut the potato and sweet potato into 1cm-thick fries, then fry in the hot oil for 5 minutes. Carefully remove from the fryer with the fryer basket or a slotted spoon and dust in the potato flour – this isn't essential, but it gives a wonderful added crispness.

Now heat the oil up to 190°C, then drop in the bacon and fry until crisp and almost over-done. Remove and drain on kitchen paper.

Cook the fries again in the hot oil for 3–4 minutes until golden and crisp. Tip into a bowl and season with salt and pepper, then lace with the paprika mayo, spring onions, cheddar and jalapeños. Finally, crumble the bacon over the top with your fingers and tuck in!

POSH DAWGS!

SERVES 4

1 onion, sliced as thinly as
    possible into whole rings
50ml whole milk
vegetable oil, for deep frying
100g plain flour
4 hot dogs (or frankfurters)
100g Red Cabbage Sauerkraut
    (page 60)
4 brioche hot-dog buns
sea salt
ketchup and French's mustard,
    to serve

A day at the circus is not complete without some nostalgic fast food. It's the food you imagine having at a circus, so why not make it nice?

Soak the onion rings in the milk for a few minutes before draining in a colander.

Heat the vegetable oil in a deep-fat fryer or heavy-based saucepan to 190°C. Toss the onions in the flour, a few at a time to avoid clumping, then fry, in batches, in the hot oil for 30 seconds, or until golden. Drain on kitchen paper and season lightly with salt.

In a small saucepan, warm up the hot dogs with the Red Cabbage Sauerkraut on the stove over low heat. Serve in the hot-dog buns with a mad squeeze of ketchup, mustard and the fried onions.

PIZZA
IN THE CHADWICK OVENS

MAKES 6 INDIVIDUAL PIZZAS

semolina, for dusting
6 x 125g balls fresh mozzarella
dried oregano, for sprinkling
handful of basil leaves
sea salt and black pepper

For the pizza dough
2 x 7g sachets dried yeast
400ml warm water
700g "00" flour
2 tsp salt

For the tomato sauce
400-g tin of good-quality
   plum tomatoes
1 garlic clove, peeled
50ml olive oil, plus extra for
   greasing

For the pizza dough, add the yeast to the warm water and stir with a balloon whisk until the yeast has dissolved. In the bowl of an electric mixer with the dough hook fitted, combine the flour and salt, then slowly pour in the yeast mixture. Knead on full blast for 10 minutes, until the dough is smooth and elastic.

Divide the dough into 6 equal pieces and roll into balls between your palms, then place on an oiled baking tray or work surface. Pop a clean, damp tea towel over the top and leave to prove for 1–2 hours until the balls have almost doubled in size.

For the tomato sauce, blend the ingredients with salt and pepper to taste, using either a stick blender or food processor.

The pizza dough should be nicely plump and pliable by now. It's time to preheat the oven – Chadwick or not! Preheat the oven to the highest temperature it will go – about 260°C if possible.

Dust a pizza paddle or stone, or if you haven't got one, a large, flat baking tray, with a small amount of semolina before you start to shape the dough. On a surface generously sprinkled with semolina, roll, toss, stretch, shape, drop – and try again if you need to... whatever it takes to get a nice thin pizza base onto the paddle or baking tray.

Once satisfied, use a ladle to smear the tomato sauce thinly over the pizza in a circular motion, then rip the mozzarella and scatter over the top, along with a sprinkle of oregano and a few torn basil leaves. Work as quickly as you can so the base doesn't stick to the paddle or baking sheet.

Now it's time to shunt the pizza in the oven – and this, too, may take some practice! As with pancakes, the first one is the most difficult. Bake the pizza for about 8–12 minutes until the pizza crust rises and toasts and the mozzarella bubbles, turning it every now and then to cook evenly. Once it is risen, charred and golden, pull it out, slice and share... or not.

Making a good pizza is both a science and an art. The dough is alive and you need to treat it as such. You need the right conditions, moisture, temperature and time. The Chadwick Oven, invented by our friend Dan Chadwick, who lives over the road from the farm, is a stovetop pizza oven that goes up to a very high temperature. We have a number of these in our pizza wagon, constantly churning out brilliantly crisp, bubbling pizzas. Obviously you can add whatever other toppings you like. Go nuts!

SALTED MAPLE POPCORN

SERVES 6

1 large bowl of plain cooked
    popcorn (cooked either in a
    microwave or in a saucepan
    with a little vegetable oil)
50g unsalted butter
50ml maple syrup, plus extra
    for drizzling
100g light brown sugar
½ tsp bicarbonate of soda
sea salt
crispy smoked bacon (optional)

An irresistible alternative to sweet or salty popcorn. This is "a bit o' both", as our Canadian bow-and-fiddle player would say! And it's even better topped with crumbled smoked bacon!

Sit a heavy baking tray on top of a damp, folded tea towel on your worktop to avoid any damage to the surface. Line the baking tray with baking parchment and tip in the popcorn, spreading it out evenly.

Melt the butter in a saucepan over a medium heat before adding the maple syrup and brown sugar. Bring to the boil and cook for a further 5 minutes until fierce bubbles appear and it begins to darken in colour. Add the bicarbonate of soda, stirring vigorously – the mix should bubble up.

Carefully pour the hot caramel over the popcorn and sprinkle with sea salt. Toss around with a metal or silicone spoon, then leave to cool.

Transfer to a bowl and, if you like, crumble over some crispy grilled bacon and drizzle with a little bit more maple syrup.

THE CARAVAN CRAWL

Every so often on tour, before a day off, the crew decide on
a crawl: a party that you can't really create anywhere else.
A 15-minute window to host a vast number of circus folk
at your bunk, wagon or caravan – complete with a theme,
nibbles and entertainment – before the bong sounds and
the flock moves on to the next abode. You learn a lot about
who you've spent the last (and next) few months of your
life with on this night. Nowhere else but here…

hangover hash

WITH POACHED EGGS AND MUSTARD, HORSERADISH AND DILL MAYO

SERVES 6 HUNGOVER
PARTY-GOERS

200g leftover roast potatoes
1 carrot
1 celery stick
1 onion
vegetable oil, for frying
300g cooked salt beef or tinned
    corn beef
1 tsp ground allspice
1 tsp smoked paprika
dash of vinegar
6 eggs
sea salt and black pepper

For the mayo
1 tsp English mustard
1 tsp horseradish sauce
handful of chopped dill
100g mayonnaise

With rationing, hash became popular in the Second World War and for some time afterwards, but has since gone out of fashion. Which is a shame, because it's both simple and wonderful. Spicy meat, fried potatoes and poached eggs – where can you go wrong? We use Moran eggs with beautifully rich yolks for this dish, which is our musical director James's favourite for cooking (usually in his undergarments) on a caravan stove.

Start dicing everything! 'Hash' comes from the French *hacher*, 'to chop'. So dice all the veg and the meat and get the veg into a hot frying pan with a drizzle of vegetable oil. Add the spices and a good turn of salt and pepper before chucking in the beef. Keep frying, giving it a stir every so often, until satisfied.

Meanwhile, for the mayo, mix the mustard, horseradish, dill and mayonnaise together with a dash of water. (This is not the time for making your own mayonnaise…)

Bring a saucepan of water to the boil with a pinch of salt and a good dash of vinegar. Turn the heat down to a simmer – you want Champagne-like bubbles – then crack in the eggs, holding them as close to the water as you can, and poach for 2–3 minutes. Remove from the water with a slotted spoon and drain on a clean tea towel or kitchen paper.

Plonk the eggs straight into the frying pan with the hash and a good coating of the loosened mayonnaise. Serve with a stack of plates and cutlery and try to contain this hangover!

GIFFORDS FISH PIE

SERVES 6

200g mussels, clams or razor
   clams, cleaned and bearded
500g salmon, cod and smoked
   haddock, diced
6–12 raw tiger prawns or
   langoustines
100ml white wine
500ml double cream
1 tbsp Dijon mustard
2 bay leaves
50g butter
2 banana shallots, thinly sliced
1 fennel bulb, thinly sliced
50g plain flour
3 hard-boiled eggs, shelled and
   chopped
juice and zest of 1 lemon
sea salt and white pepper
buttered samphire, to serve

For the mash topping
1kg floury potatoes, peeled and
   cut into chunks
50g unsalted butter, cubed
100ml double cream
2 egg yolks

For the breadcrumb topping
250g fresh breadcrumbs
small handful of dill and
   tarragon, chopped
50g unsalted butter

A nostalgic memory for me is scraping the innards of a foil tray after finishing a fish pie. What could be better – except maybe adding more shellfish... And just like a Stargazy, we pop something in there that peeks out. We use the catch of the day wherever we happen to be.

Put a saucepan over high heat until extremely hot. Throw in all the seafood and the white wine and bring to a frantic boil, then lower the heat slightly, cover with a lid and simmer for 3–4 minutes. Remove the lid, take the seafood out with a slotted spoon and put into a bowl. Keep the cooking liquor over low heat and add the cream, mustard and bay leaves and simmer for a few minutes. Reserve for later. Pick the meat from the shellfish and put all the prepared seafood in the fridge.

Melt the butter in a deep saucepan over medium heat, then add the shallots and fennel with a pinch of salt and cook for about 5 minutes, stirring often, until softened. Add the flour whilst still stirring and cook for a further 5 minutes. Now gradually ladle in the reserved cream mixture and stir until thick. Season well with salt and pepper and pick out the bay leaves. Leave to cool in a bowl in the fridge, with clingfilm pressed onto the surface of the sauce, for 2 hours until cool.

For the mash topping, boil the potatoes until you can easily stick a knife through them, then drain in a colander and give them a few minutes back in the pan over low heat to steam dry. Pass them through a ricer, moulis or just bash with a masher until smooth. Heat the butter and cream in a small pan over low heat until piping hot, then stir into the mash with the egg yolks and season well with salt and pepper. If you want to pipe it onto the pie, use a piping bag fitted with a plain nozzle.

For the breadcrumb topping, blend the ingredients together with a good pinch of salt and a turn of white pepper until the colour of the herbs comes through.

Preheat the oven to 170°C.

Add all the seafood to the cooled sauce with the chopped eggs and lemon juice and zest, and mix well. Spoon into a large pie dish, pipe or spoon over the mash, then scatter with the green breadcrumbs. Bake for 30 minutes until the crumbs start to get crispy! Serve with buttered samphire.

West Country Cassoulet

Serves 8

200g dried haricot beans
200g dried butter beans
olive oil, for frying
4 garlic cloves, finely chopped
2 onions, diced
1 small bunch of thyme (leaves picked if you don't like the stalks)
200g smoked bacon lardons
200ml red wine
6 plum tomatoes, chopped
500ml chicken stock
1 pig's trotter, cleaned
500g leftover cooked pork belly (page 33)
4–5 leftover cooked pork sausages (preferably local)
2 chicken legs
2 duck legs
½ lemon
sea salt and black pepper
spring greens, to serve

This takes me back to visiting France as a kid, and rocking up to a village in the middle of nowhere. The only place to eat would be a 'restaurant' in Madame's house that served a no-choice menu of melon and raw ham, followed by a bowl of the most amazing duck, pork and Toulouse sausage cassoulet. Near Fennells Farm in Gloucestershire we have some wonderful butchers who produce meat that's ideal for a cassoulet, so it really has to be done!

Soak the beans in plenty of water (at least 3 times the volume of beans) overnight.

The next day, preheat the oven to 120°C.

Heat a little olive oil in a large flameproof casserole dish or cast-iron pot over medium heat. Add the garlic, onions, half the thyme and the lardons, season with a good 3 or 4 pinches of salt and turns of black pepper and cook, stirring regularly, until the onions are soft and translucent. Pour in the wine and let it reduce slightly before adding the chopped tomatoes, the soaked beans and the chicken stock. Bring to the boil, then drop in the pig's trotter, cover with a lid and pop in the oven for at least 2 hours.

Cut the pork belly and sausages into 2cm chunks. Add a drizzle of oil to a frying pan over medium–high heat and fry the pork belly, sausages, chicken legs and duck legs with a little salt and pepper. Once they are all nicely browned, sink them into the cassoulet pot, cover with the lid and return to the oven for another 2 hours.

Turn the oven up to 200°C. Remove the lid from the cassoulet pot, scatter with the rest of the thyme, squeeze in the juice from the lemon half and roast for a further 30 minutes until the meat is crisp.

Serve with some spring greens, or whatever you can find on the allotment!

RUMP OF LAMB
WITH BLACK-CABBAGE SALSA VERDE

SERVES 2

2–3 heads black cabbage
  (cavolo nero)
2 garlic cloves, peeled
1 small bunch parsley, leaves
  picked
6–7 mint leaves
3 anchovies, roughly chopped
1 tbsp Dijon mustard
2 tbsp capers
squeeze of lemon juice
2 x 200g lamb rumps, skin
  removed and fat scored
sea salt and black pepper

A salsa verde made with black cabbage is the perfect way to cut through the fattiness of lamb. This works wonderfully with some braised lentils on the side.

Take the black cabbage and strip the black leaves away from the stalks. Throw the stripped leaves into a saucepan of salted boiling water and cook for 4–5 minutes, then refresh under cold running water in a sieve. Once cooled, use your hands to squeeze out as much water as possible, then put half into a food processor or blender. Add the garlic, parsley, mint, anchovies and mustard with a decent pinch of salt and blend until you have a deep green, smooth paste. Chuck in the capers, pulse until chunky and finish with a squeeze of lemon.

Preheat the oven to 200°C.

Season the lamb rumps well with salt and pepper, then place them, fat-side down, in an ovenproof frying pan over a medium–high heat until the fat has rendered, then turn over and colour the meat on all sides. Transfer to the oven and roast on a baking tray, fat-side down, for about 9 minutes. Remove from the oven and leave to rest for 5 minutes on a wire rack; the lamb will be a lovely pink.

Reheat the other half of the black cabbage in the same pan you used for the lamb with a turn of salt and pepper. Slice the rump thickly and serve with a good dousing of the salsa verde and the cabbage leaves.

SERVES 4

4 egg yolks
80g caster sugar
400ml whole milk
1 vanilla pod, split and seeds
    scraped
4 gelatine leaves, soaked in cold
    water for 15 minutes
300ml double cream
ice

For the biscotti (makes 12)
500g plain flour
310g caster sugar
½ tsp salt
½ tsp baking powder
150g mixed nuts, such as
    pistachios, hazelnuts,
    almonds, walnuts
30g soft unsalted butter
3 small eggs

For the berry compote
300g mixed berries, such as
    strawberries, raspberries and
    blackberries
50g caster sugar
peeled zest of 1 lemon
1 cinnamon stick
1 star anise

Bavarian cream, or bavarois, is a set custard, and it makes a beautifully simple dessert that needs no thrills or spills – just a spooning of berry compote and some biscotti for a nutty crunch. Even better, you can make it in advance and whip it out of the fridge when needed.

In a heatproof bowl, whisk the egg yolks and sugar together with a balloon whisk until frothy. In a saucepan, bring the milk and vanilla pod and seeds to the boil, then slowly pour into the bowl of whisked eggs and sugar, whisking constantly until incorporated. Pour back into the pan over medium heat, stirring continuously with a wooden spoon, and cook until thick enough to coat the back of the spoon. Remove from the heat, add the squeezed-out gelatine and stir until dissolved.

Meanwhile, whip the cream until soft peaks appear and leave to the side until needed. Pass the custard through a sieve into a metal or glass bowl sitting in another bowl of iced water. Stir frequently as it cools, until it just starts to thicken like blancmange, then remove from the iced water and fold in the whipped cream until you have a wonderfully light custard. Pour into four 200ml dariole moulds and chill for 2 hours until set.

For the biscotti, preheat the oven to 170°C and line a large baking tray with baking parchment.

Put the flour, sugar, salt and baking powder into the bowl of an electric mixer fitted with a whisk attachment and mix briefly to combine. Add the nuts and the soft butter, mix briefly, then add the eggs and mix on high speed to form a dough. Roll into a log and place on the baking tray, then flatten into a rectangle shape about 3cm thick. Bake for 15–20 minutes until it turns ever so slightly golden. Remove from the oven and turn the temperature down to 160°C. Leave the log to cool slightly, then slice into 1cm-thick biscuits. Lay the biscotti back on the baking tray and bake for 10–15 minutes, until lightly coloured and crisp. Leave to cool.

For the berry compote, hull and halve the strawberries, then put all the berries in a stainless-steel saucepan with the rest of the ingredients. Bring to the boil, then remove from the heat and leave to cool.

To serve, dip the bases of the Bavarian creams in hot water to loosen, then turn them out onto plates. Add a spoonful of the compote and serve with the biscotti.

BAVARIAN CREAM WITH BERRY COMPOTE AND BISCOTTI

RUM BABAS

WITH ROAST PINEAPPLE

Rum is one of our favourite tipples at the circus – and here it works brilliantly with roast pineapple and soaked through a baba. We just have to make sure it doesn't get turned into a cocktail before then...

SERVES 4

For the roast pineapple
1 pineapple
50g soft unsalted butter
150g dark brown sugar
250ml pineapple juice
50ml dark rum
1 cinnamon stick
2 star anise
1 vanilla pod, split
clotted cream, to serve

For the rum babas
80ml milk
10g dried yeast
25g caster sugar
200g strong flour, plus extra
    for dusting
1 tsp salt
1 whole egg
1 egg yolk
100g soft unsalted butter,
    cubed, plus extra for greasing

For the rum babas, warm the milk to body temperature (in a microwave or on the hob), then mix in the yeast and sugar until dissolved. Put the flour and salt in an electric mixer fitted with the dough hook. Add the yeast mixture and the whole egg and mix on a low speed until a dough begins to form. Turn the mixer up to full blast and knead for about 8 minutes until the dough is smooth and elastic. Now, with the mixer running at low speed, add the butter slowly, a cube at a time, until it is all incorporated. Cover the bowl with a clean, damp tea towel and leave the dough to prove in a warm place for about 30–40 minutes until it has doubled in size.

Grease the insides of four 75-ml dariole moulds and dust with flour. Turn the risen dough out onto a lightly floured surface and divide into 8 equal pieces. Roll each piece into a ball and sit two in each mould, one on top of the other. Leave in a warm place for about 20–30 minutes until the babas are starting to pop their heads out of the moulds.

Meanwhile, preheat the oven to 180°C.

Lightly beat the egg yolk and brush over the babas with a pastry brush. Bake for 15–20 minutes until risen and golden. Leave to cool slightly before turning out onto a wire rack.

For the roast pineapple, reduce the oven temperature to 160°C. Carve the skin off the pineapple, removing any spines with the tip of a knife but leaving the leaves intact, then put into a roasting tray. Rub with the butter and brown sugar all over. Roast for 1 hour, turning the pineapple halfway through and basting it with the juices in the tray.

Remove the pineapple from the tray and pop the tray on the hob over low heat. Pour in the pineapple juice and rum and add the cinnamon stick, star anise and vanilla pod. Simmer for 5 minutes, stirring until all the lovely caramelised sugar from the pineapple has dissolved into a syrup. Pop the babas into the liquid and baste with a spoon until soaked through, then turn off the heat and cover with foil for 5 minutes.

Serve the babas with the pineapple, a knife for carving, and a good scoop of clotted cream.

CHAPTER SEVEN

OUR REVELS NOW ARE ENDING

In a moment, the summer days seem to slip through our fingers. As they dissolve, our energy returns. In high summer, circus costumes can be a very particular form of torture: thick tights and wool jackets in a heatwave are difficult – and working in such costumes requires a kind of yogic concentration and calm. But, somewhere around the middle of August, the nights are cool again and the backstage wardrobe wagons are no longer stuffy and boiling. In fact, heaters are needed in the evenings, and the warm puffer coats and rubber boots abandoned in the summer are dug out, ready for the long hours of waiting around backstage.

On Minchinhampton Common, the nights begin to darken and soon, seemingly by some kind of cosmic twist or loophole, we are on Marlborough Common and the nights get longer, darker and damper. Our sunshine-drenched world is replaced by one festooned with glittering cobwebs, carpeted with wet grass and lit by sparkling light bulbs. It is as if we have all been dreaming a long dream together, and here, high on the chalk downs, the Big Top fluttering against a darkening sky, we suddenly wake up.

I have a sense that the company has gone wild; it feels like we have lived a lifetime in our little caravans on grassy fields, linked to the outside world only by a radio or the screen of a mobile phone. And in Marlborough – a proper, bustling little market town with pubs, cafés, a good market and even a nightclub – we have to rehabilitate ourselves to normal life again. We fall upon Pino's restaurant, assured of professional, gentle Italian hospitality and a late-night bar. I buy the children's back-to-school shoes in the Clarks shop on the high street. There is a sense that, somewhere in the distance, winter is waiting.

Strange things have happened on Marlborough Common and, like all our regular grounds, it is full of memories. It is impossible to drive past any of our stands and ignore the strange sensation of past, present and future meeting – invisible and yet so potent. The night, years ago, when the strange French horse trainers, who had been with us for the season, ran away in the night, taking their horses and our tack room with them. The awful show when a lovely Hungarian trapeze artist collapsed in the ring from a snapped Achilles tendon. The night the tent broke.

I HAVE A SENSE THAT THE COMPANY HAS GONE WILD; IT FEELS LIKE WE HAVE LIVED A LIFETIME IN OUR LITTLE CARAVANS ON GRASSY FIELDS, LINKED TO THE OUTSIDE WORLD ONLY BY A RADIO OR THE SCREEN OF A MOBILE PHONE.

Dawns spent exercising the spotted horses and Dalmatians together. The audiences who came by microlight, Rolls Royce, horse and cart, or on foot. The day when Vivienne Westwood arrived – a tiny lady with bright orange hair and a stern manner – and we stood in the rain and talked business, and I remember Nancy's face was painted gold.

When I walk across the common I am aware of the generations of children in my own family who have grown up with the circus. My sisters' children are loyal (hardened) circus visitors who transitioned from toddlers, chasing the circus chickens or having a ride on one of the horses, to starry-eyed youngsters and nonchalant teenagers, then keen gap-year helpers and young adults. Emma's oldest daughter, Lil, has even become a circus professional herself. My own children, Red and Cecil Gifford, who at the time of writing this are nine years old, have grown up on these various circus grounds across the west country. Life has been played out on these greens: marriages have started and ended; babies have been conceived, born and brought up. Life will continue to unfold, as will the circus, which has a life of its own and its own secrets – it's as if the walls of the tent itself has ears, memory and skin-like sensations.

Now that the outside air is cool, suppers in the circus restaurant are more hearty. Ols and his team serve freshly made breads, still warm from the oven, alongside roast duck or venison hotpot. The feasting carries on until late and things can get raucous. People are coming home from holidays, and a night at the circus feels like their last fling of the summer.

LIFE HAS BEEN PLAYED OUT ON THESE GREENS: MARRIAGES HAVE STARTED AND ENDED; BABIES HAVE BEEN CONCEIVED, BORN AND BROUGHT UP.

FOCACCIA

MAKES 1 LOAF

350ml lukewarm water
150ml olive oil
2 x 7g sachets of dried yeast
500g strong white flour
2 tsp salt
4 sprigs rosemary, leaves picked
2 garlic cloves

One of our staples. The rosemary and garlic make it a firm favourite on our table, perfect for dunking in balsamic vinegar or spreading with butter. You can use any number of herbs to flavour the bread, but we like to keep it simple with rosemary from wherever you can pilfer it from.

Mix the water, 50ml of the olive oil, and the yeast with a spoon until dissolved. Pile the flour and salt into a mound on your work surface, then make a well in the middle. Slowly add the yeast liquid, using your fingers to draw in the flour and bring everything together to make a dough. Once fully incorporated, knead the dough for 10 minutes until smooth. Drape a clean, damp tea towel over the dough and leave for at least 20 minutes until doubled in size. Transfer the dough to a well oiled baking tray and flatten out with your palms to try to cover the tray.

Preheat the oven to 220°C.

In a food processor, briefly pulse the rosemary leaves, garlic and remaining olive oil together. Rub over the focaccia, pushing your fingers into the dough to create little wells for the oil. Bake for 30–40 minutes until golden, then leave to cool on a wire rack.

SODA BREAD

MAKES 1 LOAF

250g plain flour
250g multigrain flour, plus extra
   for dusting
1 tsp bicarbonate of soda
10g salt
about 450ml buttermilk

Soda bread smells almost as good as it tastes, and is so very easy to make. Imagine what a treat this is to wake up to on a crisp autumnal morning, with butter melting into the still-warm bread.

Preheat the oven to 200°C.

In a large bowl, mix the flours with the bicarbonate of soda and salt. Start slowly adding the buttermilk, working it in with your fingertips and adding just enough to form a light dough.

Roll the dough into a ball and dust with a little more multigrain flour, then place on a flour-dusted baking tray. Use a sharp knife to score a cross in the top. Bake for 30 minutes, or until it sounds hollow when you tap on the base of the loaf.

SWEET POTATO BREAD

MAKES 1 LOAF

375g sweet potatoes, unpeeled
and cut into chunks
2 x 7g sachets of dried yeast
375g strong white flour, plus
extra for dusting
2 tsp salt

You would think this was sourdough from the look and taste of it, as the sweet potatoes give it a brilliantly earthy flavour. This is one of the more unusual breads we make, and is best eaten with some salted butter.

Put the sweet potatoes in a saucepan of water, bring to the boil and boil for 10–15 minutes until you can easily prod a knife through them. Drain but reserve the cooking liquor. Put the potatoes back in the pan over low heat to steam dry and let the cooking liquor cool to just warm.

Measure out 50ml of the cooking liquor and stir in the dried yeast. Leave for 10 minutes until the mix starts to go frothy.

Lightly mash the potatoes in a bowl just using your hands, add the yeast mixture, flour and salt and form into a dough. Knead the dough on a lightly floured surface for 10 minutes until soft and slightly elastic, return to the bowl, drape a clean, damp tea towel over and leave for 30–40 minutes until doubled in side.

Turn out the dough on a lightly floured surface and mould into a roughly oval loaf. Place on a flour-dusted baking tray and leave to rest for a further 20 minutes.

Meanwhile, preheat the oven to 220°C.

Use a sharp knife to score ridges in the top of the loaf. Fill a heatproof cup with water and place it on the lowest shelf of the oven to create some steam – this helps to develop a good crust on the loaf. Slide the baking tray onto the middle shelf and bake the bread for 20–30 minutes until the crust is quite dark and sounds hollow when you tap the base. Leave to cool on a wire rack.

Charcoal Grissini

MAKES 20–30 GRISSINI

7g sachet of dried yeast
1 tsp caster sugar
175ml lukewarm water
360g plain flour, plus extra for
    dusting
15g activated charcoal powder
2 tsp salt
25ml olive oil
knob of butter

Originating from Turin in northern Italy, grissini make a brilliant way to start a meal. These breadsticks are perfect for dipping or to wrap in prosciutto, and the charcoal gives them a satisfyingly bitter edge. You can find activated charcoal in any healthfood shop. Just don't forget to set a time for baking the grissini – you'll never know if they're burnt!

Stir the yeast and sugar into the warm water and let sit for 10 minutes until the liquid begins to froth.

Put the flour, charcoal, salt, olive oil and butter into the bowl of an electric mixer fitted with a dough hook. Add the yeast mixture and mix on low speed until a dough forms. Turn the mixer up to high speed and knead for 10 minutes until smooth and elastic. Remove from the mixer, drape a clean, damp tea towel over the dough and leave to prove for 30–40 minutes until doubled in size.

On a lightly floured surface, mould the dough into a rectangle and, using a sharp knife, slice the dough into sticks about 2cm thick. Then use your hands to roll the sticks out further until about 20cm long. Place the grissini on flour-dusted baking trays and leave to prove for a further 10 minutes.

Preheat the oven to 170°C.

Bake for 10–15 minutes until firm and crisp.

PURPLE SPROUTING BROCCOLI

WITH SOFT-BOILED EGGS AND HOLLANDAISE

SERVES 2–4

3 eggs
300g purple sprouting broccoli,
    ends trimmed
knob of butter
1 shallot, sliced into thin rings
sea salt and black pepper
rocket and smoked paprika,
    to serve

For the hollandaise sauce
2 tbsp Hollandaise Vinegar
    (page 58)
2 egg yolks
150g unsalted butter, melted
squeeze of lemon juice

For this simple dish, we rely entirely on the quality of our ingredients. Sprouting broccoli is already nearing the end of its season when we start touring, so we have to get in quick. We use Arlington White eggs from Cacklebean Farm, which is just down the road from us – paired with the lovely butter from Woefuldane Dairy in Minchinhampton: the sunset-coloured yolks give the hollandaise a wonderful glow. This is great to eat at any time of day.

For the hollandaise sauce, get a saucepan of water up to a simmer. Grab a heatproof bowl that will sit nicely on top of the saucepan, making sure the simmering water does not touch the base of the bowl. Put the Hollandaise Vinegar and egg yolks in the bowl over the pan of simmering water and whisk vigorously until the egg yolks start to cook and the mixture thickens. Once the whisk creates ribbons in the mixture, remove from the heat but keep whisking for another 30 seconds.

Trickle in the melted butter very slowly from a jug, still whisking constantly. Add the lemon juice and season well with salt and pepper, then keep it somewhere warm while you cook the eggs and broccoli.

Bring a saucepan of water to the boil with a good pinch of salt, gently lower in the eggs and boil for 5 minutes. Remove from the pan and peel whilst still hot, then cut in half. In the same pan, chuck in the broccoli and cook for 3–4 minutes until the stems go slightly limp. Remove and set aside.

Drop the knob of butter into a frying pan over medium heat and fry the shallot rings until just starting to turn golden. Add the cooked broccoli and toss about in the pan with a turn of salt and pepper.

Serve with the boiled eggs, hollandaise sauce, a few rocket leaves and a pinch of smoked paprika.

We like to serve this hearty Scottish soup with a dense stottie cake and some pease pudding from over the border. We generally have a stottie sarnie for Move Day, with some cheddar, smoked ham and pease pudding – sustenance for the long haul. To 'stot' in the native Geordie tongue means to bounce, so the bread does need to be quite dense. Dan Brown our wonderful chef de partie has taught us a lot about the North East, and this is a homage to him! Whey, aye!

SERVES 6

1.5 litres whole milk
500ml double cream
2 bay leaves
2 carrots, finely diced
1 onion, finely diced
500g naturally smoked haddock
2 large waxy potatoes, peeled and cut into 1cm cubes
1 tbsp Dijon mustard
3 leeks, washed and finely diced
small handful of chopped chives, to serve

For the pease pudding
300g yellow split peas
2 garlic cloves, bashed
50ml rapeseed oil
juice of ½ lemon
50g walnuts, toasted
sea salt and black pepper

For the stottie cakes
250ml warm water
10g dried yeast
1 tsp caster sugar
400g strong white flour
1 tsp salt
1 tsp white pepper
1 egg, lightly beaten
50g oats

CULLEN SKINK WITH STOTTIE CAKES AND PEASE PUDDING

For the pease pudding, put the split peas in a saucepan and cover with cold water. Add the whole garlic cloves and cook over low heat for 1 hour, or until the peas are tender. Drain and tip into a food processor. With the machine running, slowly drizzle in the oil. When you have a fairly smooth purée, add the lemon juice and toasted walnuts, blitz briefly and season well with salt and pepper.

For the stottie cakes, put the warm water, yeast, sugar and 2 tablespoons of the flour in an electric mixer fitted with a dough hook and give it a good whisk just with a fork for now. Leave for 10 minutes – the yeast should have activated and the mix should start to froth. Now add the rest of the flour, the salt and white pepper and knead for 10–15 minutes until smooth and elastic. Remove from the mixer, drape a clean, damp tea towel over the dough and leave for 20–30 minutes until doubled in size. Preheat the oven to 200°C.

Divide the risen dough into 6 pieces, roll into balls and lay out on a floured baking tray. Brush the tops with the beaten egg and dust with the oats, then leave to prove for a further 20 minutes. Before baking, poke your finger in the centre of each ball for the trademark hole, then bake for 15 minutes. Turn the oven off and leave the stottie cakes in for a further 10 minutes to allow them to gather moisture. Remove from the oven and leave to cool on a wire rack.

The soup is wonderfully simple. In a large saucepan, bring the milk, cream, bay leaves, carrots and onion to a simmer, then drop in the haddock and cook for 5 minutes. Lift out the fish and, when it is cool enough to handle, flake the flesh, discarding any skin and bones, and set aside until needed.

Add the potatoes and mustard to the liquid in the pan and cook for about 5 minutes, then add the leeks and simmer for 10–15 minutes until all the vegetables are tender. Season the soup with salt and pepper to taste, then add the fish and stir gently to heat through. Finish with a sprinkling of chives.

Ladle the cullen skink into bowls, then spread the pease pudding like butter over the stottie cakes and dunk into the soup as you eat.

VENISON HOTPOT

WITH CHESTNUTS AND CHOCOLATE

SERVES 6

1kg venison, cubed
3 sprigs thyme, leaves picked
4 juniper berries, lightly crushed
vegetable oil, for frying
100g unsalted butter
3 onions, thinly sliced
50g plain flour
500ml beef or venison stock
50g dark chocolate, finely grated
1 venison marrowbone (optional)
100g chestnuts (fresh and shelled, or precooked)
1kg large waxy potatoes, peeled
sea salt and black pepper

We know we're nearing the end of the season when we get to a venison hotpot – and where better to make it than Marlborough? Andrews, our butcher there, sells locally shot venison and we reap the benefits in this classic dish.

Rub the venison all over with the thyme leaves, juniper berries and salt and pepper. Heat a little vegetable oil in a heavy-based frying pan over a medium heat and, working in small batches, sear the venison until nicely browned. Set aside in a bowl.

In the same pan, melt half of the butter, add the onions and fry until soft and translucent before sprinkling in the flour. Cook, stirring, for 3–4 minutes, then pour in the stock together with any juices from the venison bowl, stirring well to ensure there are no lumps. Return the venison to the pan and stir in the chocolate, then remove from the heat.

Preheat the oven to 140°C.

Melt the remaining butter. Clean up the venison marrowbone, if using, and place it upright in the centre of a deep, round casserole dish. Spoon in the contents of the frying pan and crumble over the chestnuts. Slice the potatoes very thinly with a knife or on a mandoline. Start arranging them in a spiral on top of the casserole, brushing each layer with the melted butter and seasoning with salt and pepper. Keep going until you've used up all the spuds. Put the casserole in the oven and cook, uncovered, for 2–3 hours.

When it's done, the meat should be tender and the potato crisp – perfect as the weather starts to turn autumnal.

This is the Giffords version of Chinese crispy duck with pancakes, and it's rather moreish. The brining is very important here – it flavours the duck and allows the skin to get lovely and crisp. Serve with a pile of crêpes, the refreshing rémoulade and sweet plum sauce.

SERVES 6

1 x 2kg duck
100ml honey
sea salt and white pepper

For the brine
1 litre apple juice
100g black treacle
100g dark brown sugar
150g salt
3 garlic cloves, crushed
3 star anise

For the crêpes
200g plain flour
1 tsp salt
2 eggs
470ml whole milk

For the plum sauce
200g plums, stones removed
60g caster sugar
1 tsp ground cinnamon

For the rémoulade
1 celeriac
100g mayonnaise (see page 139 for homemade)
1 tbsp Dijon mustard
1 tbsp wholegrain mustard
squeeze of lemon juice

Put all the ingredients for the brine into a stainless-steel saucepan and bring to the boil, then pour into a deep bowl or plastic tub large enough to hold the duck and leave to cool. Once the brine is cold, immerse the duck in it and leave in the fridge for 1–2 days, turning over every so often.

Preheat the oven to 140°C. Remove the duck from the brine, pat dry with kitchen paper and sit on a wire rack in a deep roasting tray. Cover tightly with foil and roast for 3 hours.

Meanwhile, make the batter for the crêpes. Combine the flour and salt in a bowl. Whisk together the eggs and milk, then slowly whisk into the flour until you have a thin batter. Leave to rest in the fridge for at least 30 minutes.

For the plum sauce, put all the ingredients and 100ml water in a stainless-steel saucepan and simmer gently for about 15 minutes or until the plums are soft. Mash to a rough purée with a fork.

For the rémoulade, peel the celeriac, then either grate it or use a knife or mandoline to cut it into very thin strips. Place in a colander, salt lightly and mix well, then leave to drain for 15 minutes. Use your hands to squeeze out as much moisture as possible, then tip the celeriac into a bowl. Stir in the mayonnaise, both mustards and the lemon juice. The rémoulade should have quite a punch to it!

When the duck has had 3 hours, remove it and increase the oven temperature to 210°C. Take off the foil and baste the duck with the cooking juices in the tray. Pour the rest of the juices from the roasting tray into a small saucepan and set aside. Season the duck with a sprinkle of salt, then return to the oven and roast for 20–30 minutes, until wonderfully crisp.

Add the honey to the roasting juices in the saucepan and simmer for 10–15 minutes until reduced to a syrupy glaze.

Now bash out as many pancakes as you can from the batter. Heat a drizzle of vegetable oil in a non-stick frying pan and cook each pancake briefly on both sides over medium heat.

Paint the duck with the honey glaze, then jam a couple of forks into it, ready to shred the crisp skin and tender meat. Serve with a stack of the crêpes, the rémoulade and the plum sauce… Time to get messy!

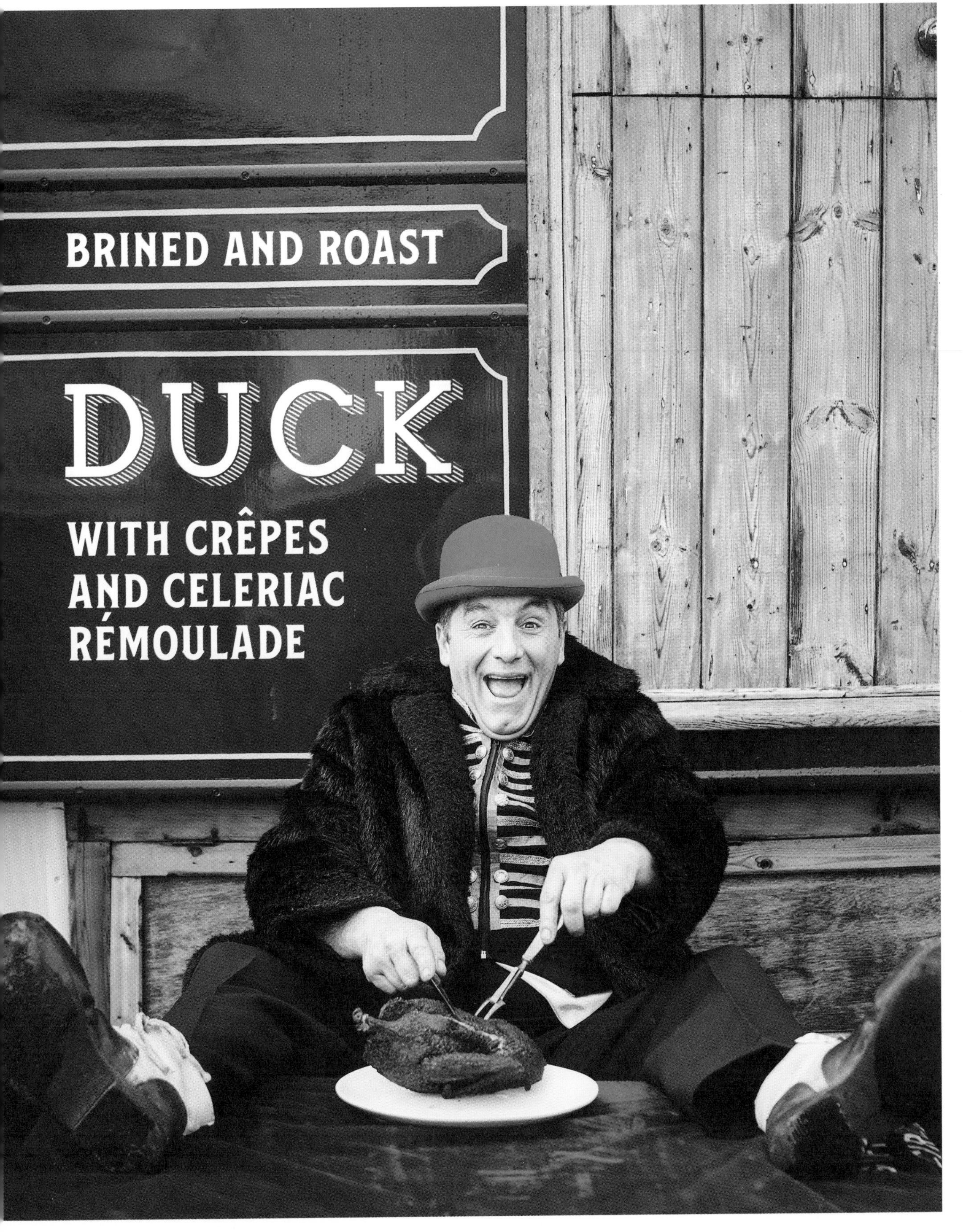

BRINED AND ROAST

DUCK

WITH CRÊPES
AND CELERIAC
RÉMOULADE

SHEPHERD'S SHANK PIE

SERVES 6

1 lamb shank
500g lamb shoulder meat, diced
vegetable oil, for frying
150ml red wine
500g minced lamb
1 large onion, diced
2 garlic cloves, crushed
1 leek, washed and sliced
2 carrots, diced
3 plum tomatoes, peeled and
    chopped
3 sprigs of thyme, leaves picked
2 bay leaves
sea salt and black pepper

For the mash
1kg floury potatoes, peeled and
    cut into chunks
50g unsalted butter
100ml double cream
2 egg yolks

Sheer nostalgia – coming home from school to the alluring smell of onions and garlic and the warmth and buzz of the oven. The lamb shank gives the pie hidden depths of flavour and another texture. You have to run a fork through the mash for texture, and you can sprinkle some cheese or breadcrumbs over it before it goes in the oven, if you like, but it's pretty good as it is.

Season the lamb shank and shoulder meat well with salt and pepper. Heat a little oil in a deep, cast-iron pot with a lid and brown the meat over high heat. When it is nicely browned all over, pour in the red wine and use a wooden spoon to scrape up any caramelised bits from the pot, then transfer the meat and wine to a bowl. Wipe out the pot, then add a little more oil and brown the minced lamb. Add the onion and garlic, turn the heat down to low–medium and cook for 10 minutes until the onion is soft and translucent, then add the leek, carrots, tomatoes, thyme and bay leaves. Return the shank and shoulder meat to the pot, along with any juices from the bowl. Pour in enough water to cover, leaving just the tip of the shank bone sitting proudly in the middle. Bring to the boil then turn down to a simmer, cover with the lid and cook for 2½ hours, or until the meat starts to pull away from the shank.

Preheat the oven to 180°C.

For the mash, boil the potatoes until cooked, then drain and mash with a masher, ricer or mouli. In a small saucepan over low heat, melt the butter in the cream, then stir into the mashed potato. Season with salt and pepper and finally add the egg yolks, mixing well until smooth.

Spoon the mash around the shank and use a fork to make a tower, just like you did with your mash as a kid. Cook in the oven for 20 minutes until the mash is golden, then serve up, settle in on the sofa and stick the telly on.

SPICED BABY MONKFISH TAILS

WITH MUSSEL CREAM AND
ROAST BABY PARSNIPS

SERVES 6

1 star anise
1 tsp cumin seeds
1 tsp coriander seeds
1 tsp nigella seeds
2 tsp garam masala
6 baby monkfish tails
500g baby parsnips
vegetable oil, for frying
500g mussels, scrubbed and
   de-bearded
100ml white wine
2 shallots, thinly sliced
2 garlic cloves, thinly sliced
a 200-g tin of coconut cream
handful of coriander, chopped
2 red chillies, thinly sliced
sea salt

When the circus has been put to bed for the winter, we like to travel the world as much as we can. We love to bring back memories of the markets and restaurants we've visited and the meals we've eaten, like this one. Meaty monkfish takes on Indian spices beautifully, as do the mussels. Try to find baby parsnips, if you can – they're a lot sweeter and you can get them much crisper.

In a small, dry frying pan over medium heat, toast all the whole spices until they start to pop and smoke slightly. Chuck them straight into a spice grinder or blender with the garam masala and whizz to a fine powder. Dust the monkfish with half of this spice mix and a good pinch of salt and leave to marinate for at least 30 minutes.

Preheat the oven to 180°C.

Blanch the baby parsnips in a saucepan of boiling water for 3 minutes, then drain and tip into a roasting tray. Drizzle with oil and season with salt, then roast for 10–15 minutes until crisp and golden brown.

Briefly sear the monkfish in a frying pan over high heat with a little oil, then roast on another baking tray in the oven for 10 minutes until the flesh is almost coming off the bone.

Meanwhile, throw the mussels into a very, very hot saucepan, and when you hear a loud sizzle, add the wine, shallots and garlic and clamp on the lid. Cook for about 2–3 minutes, until the shells open up, then remove the mussels and set them aside in a bowl. Discard any mussels that remain closed.

Add the remaining spice mix to the saucepan, along with a pinch of salt and the coconut cream. Let it simmer and reduce by half, then return the mussels to the pan and stir through some chopped coriander.

Serve the monkfish with the crispy parsnips and the mussel cream. Finish with a good scattering of chillies and some more coriander.

SPICED PANNA COTTA
WITH BAKED APPLES

SERVES 4

2 bramley apples, peeled, cored and sprinkled with sugar

For the spiced panna cotta
6 gelatine leaves
250ml whole milk
250ml double cream
50g caster sugar
2 cinnamon sticks
knob of ginger, sliced
2 star anise
250g mascarpone
ice

For the pastry
350g self-raising flour, plus extra for dusting
100g vegetable suet
pinch of salt
1 whole egg
100ml whole milk
50g golden syrup
1 egg yolk, for glazing

For the sauce
100g dark brown sugar
25ml dark rum
100g raisins
1 cinnamon stick
1 vanilla pod, split

Baked apples are delicious, especially when wrapped in a rich, sweet pastry and served with a spiced panna cotta. We love seeing what we can find in different ethnic shops and supermarkets wherever we go, and not only when we're travelling: the cinnamon bark we get from a Turkish vendor in Gloucester is wonderful and tastes so different from the small quills you get from the supermarket.

For the spiced panna cotta, soak the gelatine in cold water for 10 minutes. Put the milk, cream, sugar, cinnamon, ginger and star anise in a saucepan and bring to the boil. Add the mascarpone and the squeezed-out gelatine leaves, stirring to dissolve. Pass through a fine sieve into a metal or plastic bowl, then sit this bowl in another bowl filled with ice to cool the mixture quickly, stirring every now and then until it begins to thicken. Pour into four 200ml bowls and refrigerate for about 2 hours until set.

For the pastry, put the dry ingredients into the bowl of an electric mixer fitted with the dough hook. In a small bowl, mix together the whole egg, milk and golden syrup, then, with the machine running at a medium speed, slowly pour into the dry ingredients and keep mixing until you have a smooth dough. Use your hands to shape it into a log, then wrap in clingfilm and leave to rest in the fridge for 30 minutes.

Preheat the oven to 190°C.

Roll out the pastry on a lightly floured surface into thin circles and wrap the apples, trimming off any excess pastry and making sure the apple will stand up straight. Seal with your fingers at the bottom. With a brush, glaze every last millimetre of the pastry with the egg yolk. Leave to rest in the fridge for 10 minutes.

For the sauce, place all the ingredients (except the raisins) in a saucepan with 100ml water and bring to a simmer. Chuck in the raisins, remove from the heat and leave to cool.

Bake the apples for 15 minutes, just until the pastry goes golden – any longer and the apples will burst!

Briefly dip each panna cotta bowl into hot water to release it, then turn out and serve with a good dousing of the sauce and half of a baked apple each.

PEAR AND BLACKCURRANT AUTUMN BIG TOP

SERVES 8

500g pears, peeled and cored
100g light brown sugar
1 cinnamon stick
50g blackcurrants, stalks removed
6–8 slices white bread
100g unsalted butter

For the meringue

3 egg whites, at room temperature
115g caster sugar
115g icing sugar

You know a summer pudding – well, we've moved on a season and gone autumnal with pears and blackcurrants. We make this like a charlotte, in a mould, so the bread goes nice and crispy underneath its cloak of baked meringue. It's rather naughty and lovely with a jug of thick custard.

Put the pears in a saucepan with the sugar and cinnamon stick and stew over low heat for about 15 minutes until the pears start breaking down. Add the blackcurrants, then remove the compote from the heat and set aside.

Preheat the oven to 180°C.

Slice the crusts off the bread, then lightly fry one side of each slice in the butter in a frying pan. Begin lining a round ovenproof pie dish (about 20–23cm) with the bread, placing them fried-side down, just as you would for a summer pudding. Once the mould is completely lined, spoon in the compote, then cover with more slices of bread until bulging, this time placing them fried-side up. Bake for 20 minutes until you see the butter bubbling around the edges. Remove from the oven and leave to cool for 10 minutes before carefully turning out onto a plate.

Increase the oven temperature to 220°C.

For the meringue, in an electric mixer, whisk the egg whites and cream of tartar until the whites begin to froth and are almost at the soft-peak stage, then begin slowly tapping in the caster sugar, while still whisking. Keep whisking until the meringue is super thick, then remove the bowl from the mixer. Gradually sift in the icing sugar, folding it in gently and ensuring there are no lumps of sugar left.

Pipe the meringue all over the top of the pudding in small peaks, just as you would for a baked Alaska. Either bake for 10 minutes or blast the topping with a blowtorch until golden.

CHAPTER EIGHT

THE LAST SHOW

Time contracts and vanishes.

Dark evenings turn into cold nights, and before we know it, we are back at Fennells Farm and it is like rehearsal time again, only in reverse. Soon we will be playing the last show, taking down the tent and saying our goodbyes to each other, like a family parting forever. As the last show approaches, a strange metamorphosis occurs: the props and costumes we have been carrying with us all season, lovingly maintaining and treasuring them like precious jewels, magically turn back into something else. The sardine that has been carried aloft in a quasi-religious parade, swathed in black lace and carefully hung in the back tent, is suddenly once more just a battered bit of painted papier-mâché. The bag that has held cut carrots for the Shetland ponies – a scrap of vintage material lined in waterproof cloth – and which I have guarded vigilantly all season, is suddenly a slightly smelly, dirty bit of fabric and is instantly lost.

In the same way, a thousand small rituals, friendships, incidental backstage choreographies and characters also vanish. In fact, as quickly as we put the show together, so we end it. The last show is always a whirlwind of confetti, flowers, hugs and tears, and we all watch each other's acts with a valedictory passion.

With his unfailing sense of occasion, Ols prepares goulash. This is inspired by one of our horsemen, Attila, who is a Hungarian Csikós – a traditional horseman. Of all the surviving stockmen cultures, theirs is among the most beautiful and complete. Their home is the Great Hungarian Plain (Hortobágy), where the grasslands are endless and unfenced. They traditionally wear long, flowing indigo robes and they train their horses with a quiet, patient kindness. They take pride in cooking goulash on a tripod hanging over an open fire. It's a brilliant dish for an outdoor occasion, and works so well at autumn festivals and feasts.

I love combining this Central European ritual with the very Anglo-Saxon apple-based rituals surrounding Halloween and the autumn equinox. Impromptu fun and festivities are at the heart of Giffords Circus. Without my mother's passion for family parties, where all the costumes, props, games and food were homemade, it is possible that Giffords Circus would never have happened at all. The sacred apple is baked, bobbed or crumbled, or simply gathered by the armful for decoration. My children and the other circus children make toffee apples with windfalls from the neighbour's tree, and the sweet crunch and sharp flesh seem to signify the end of the sun's warmth and the first of the frosts.

WITHOUT MY MOTHER'S PASSION FOR FAMILY PARTIES, WHERE ALL THE COSTUMES, PROPS, GAMES AND FOOD WERE HOMEMADE, IT IS POSSIBLE THAT GIFFORDS CIRCUS WOULD NEVER HAVE HAPPENED AT ALL.

Now our quarrelled-and-made-up, in-and-out-of-love, global circus family steel themselves for the goodbyes – and the end of something that no amount of group chats, messages and reconnections will ever revive. The end of the season is the end of the season. It has an absolute finality. The dream ends. There is drama and change in the weather. The temperature drops. We all turn back into something other than our tour persona. It is an intense relief and, at the same time, it is heartbreaking.

In the quiet weeks following the season, when the music ends, the generator stops humming, the global village is disbanded, and equipment and the last wagon are put to bed. Friends, lovers and comrades are waved sadly away – there is a saying in the circus, "I love you honey, but the season's over." There is nothing left to do but get some much needed rest and think of the spring and the re-awakening of the circus dream.

THE LAST SHOW IS ALWAYS A WHIRLWIND OF CONFETTI, FLOWERS, HUGS AND TEARS.

CSIKÓS GOULASH

SERVES 6–8

2 red peppers
6 plum tomatoes
1kg beef brisket, cut into 5cm
    chunks
50g plain flour
2 tsp smoked paprika
1 tsp salt
1 tsp white pepper
100g unsalted butter
2 garlic cloves, crushed
1 large white onion, sliced
2 bay leaves
3 juniper berries, lightly crushed
2 red chillies, sliced
500ml beef stock
soured cream and chopped
    parsley, to serve

For many years, this has been our legendary circus dish, originally made by the Hungarians you'd regularly see casually riding two horses around site at once. A perfect note for when the weather starts to change and everyone needs a comforting lift. We usually serve this on the closing night of the tour before the alcohol starts to flow.

Char the red peppers directly over the flame of your hob (or char them under a hot grill). When they are cool enough to handle, peel off the skins and tear the flesh into strips. Score the base of the tomatoes, then put in a pan of boiling water from the kettle for a few minutes so that the skins start to peel off. Run under cold water, peel off the skins and roughly chop the flesh.

Dust the brisket in the flour seasoned with the paprika, salt and pepper. Melt the butter in a hot cauldron or cast-iron pot and brown the meat evenly. Once the meat has coloured all over, remove and set aside. Add the garlic, onion, bay leaves, juniper berries and chillies to the pot. When the onion is soft and golden, get the brisket back in, along with the red peppers and tomatoes. Pour in the beef stock, cover with a lid and stew for 2–3 hours while the fire crackles away.

Once the meat is tender, serve the goulash with a dollop of soured cream and some chopped parsley.

Acknowledgements

There are so many people who have made this book possible, who made it a wonderful creative process and to whom we are truly grateful for their support, wisdom and guidance.

Firstly Céline Hughes, who gave us this chance to tell our story and for her cool patience and professionalism in the process. To Nikki Ellis, who's had the impossibly difficult task of sifting through a gallery of 10,000 photos to create this stunning book (and witnessed us on the caravan crawl). And to the entire Quadrille team who made this project seamless – a tough feat with a travelling circus. A massive thanks to David Loftus, the king of his trade – graceful, humble and a wonderful companion throughout – who saw all sides of us during this time.

To Toti Gifford, to whom we owe so much, who believed in us and who should have fired someone long ago but didn't! Our best friend and our creator. Thank you.

To Cal McCrystal, without whom we would never have been so silly, so outrageous or so creative – not just in the kitchen but also leaning out of a puppet hatch.

Our most heartfelt appreciation to the whole Sauce team, past and present. They all helped with the shoots, made the stories and put up with everything that was thrown at them: David Cross, Joseph Limbrick, Daniel Brown, Jack Bull, Tom Cross, George Thomas, Joe Halas, Richard Gaughan, Jack Hart, Sam Alexander, Pip Palmer, Nathan Flowers, Mike Flowers and Annabelle Edkins, to name but a few. Our wonderful front-of-house team, who broke the rules to eat in their costumes for the shot on pages 184–5. Amy Goodwin, who hand-painted the incredible book cover and also, with the Art Department had a drink on a hill! To Annie Rigg, Ursula Georgeson, Linda Berlin and Faye Wears who had the stylistic flare to make things look as wonderful and outrageous as they do.

And now to the performers who were forced to eat! Alan "Tweedy" Digweed for pie throwing, Nancy Trotter Landry for honey drizzling, Lil Rice for brownie chomping, Jan Erik Brenner for duck munching and James Keay for cooking in his underwear. Heartfelt thanks also go to: Michael Fletcher, Pozo and the Beautiful People, the Curatola brothers Emanuel and Giuseppe, Dennis Remnev, Tatyana Ozhiganova, Anna Rastova, Jacob D'Eustachio who fill this book with wonder. The ring boys and usherettes for their invaluable work and the Giffords Circus band for providing the soundtrack to this crazy place.

We cannot forget those that pull the strings and their involvement in everything: Tessa Carnegie, Emma Bradshaw, Kelly Rumbelow, Louisa Birkin, Gervase Webb, Mathew Cornelius, Harriet Irving, Willie Athill, Victoria Alywin and Lara Skowanska.

Everywhere we go, our wonderful suppliers, farms, butchers, fishmongers, greengrocers and loyalty-box fillers go out of their way to supply us in the oddest of places. To each and every one of you, thank you.

A huge all-encompassing hug to Red and Cecil Gifford, the Chadwicks, the Digweeds and Daniela Ghionea – all integral to life on tour. And lastly to Allegra McEvedy and our agent Rosemary Scoular, without whom this book would never have happened.

INDEX

Publishing Director Sarah Lavelle
Senior Commissioning Editor Céline Hughes
Design and Art Direction Nikki Ellis
Hand-painted Front Cover Artwork Amy Goodwin
Photographer David Loftus
Food Stylists Ols Halas and Annie Rigg
Prop Stylists Linda Berlin and Faye Wears
Head of Production Stephen Lang
Production Controller Nikolaus Ginelli

Published in 2020 by Quadrille,
an imprint of Hardie Grant Publishing

Quadrille
52–54 Southwark Street
London SE1 1UN
quadrille.com

Cataloguing in Publication Data: a catalogue record for this
book is available from the British Library.

Text © Nell Gifford and Ols Halas 2020
Design, layout and photography © Quadrille 2020

ISBN 978 1 78713 413 3

Printed in China

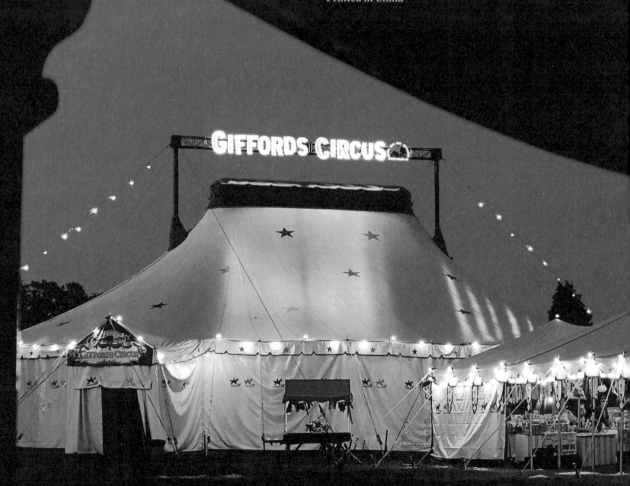